D0771118

The Galapagos Archipelago

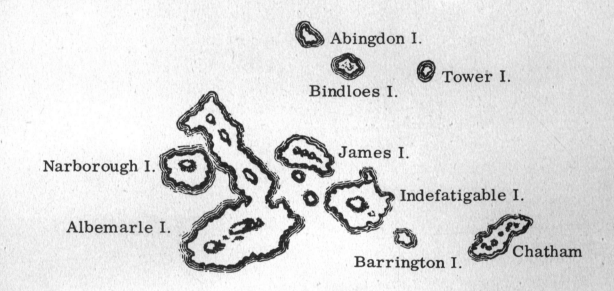

Culpepper I.

Wenman I.

60 Miles

Abingdon I.

Bindloes I.

Tower I.

Narborough I.

James I.

Indefatigable I.

Albemarle I.

Barrington I.

Chatham

Charles I.

Hood's I

DARWIN'S FORGOTTEN WORLD

DARWIN'S
FORGOTTEN
WORLD

GALLERY BOOKS
An imprint of W.H. Smith Publishers Inc.
112 Madison Avenue
New York, New York 10016
A Bison Book

4

Published by
Gallery Books
A Division of W.H. Smith Publishers Inc.
112 Madison Avenue
New York, New York 10016
USA.

Produced by
Bison Books Corp.
15 Sherwood Place
Greenwich, CT. 06830
USA.

Copyright © 1978 Bison Books Corp.

All rights reserved. No part of this book may
be reproduced, or transmitted in any form or by
any means without written permission from the Publisher.

ISBN 0–8317–2105–7

Printed in Hong Kong

10 9 8 7 6 5 4 3 2

Contents

List of color illustrations

Inset page 65: The highly colored marine iguana, found only on Hood Island.
Page 66/67 Marine iguanas, crabs and seals live happily side-by-side on Fernandina Island.
Inset: Co-existence on Hood Island.
Page 68/69 Clustered together, the marine iguanas often have to walk over each other and are well adapted for climbing the difficult rock face, on Fernandina Island *(spread)* and Punta Espinosa *(inset)*.
Page 70/71 A lonely marine iguana basks in the sun on a rock off Fernandina Island.
Page 72/73 The ugly brown Galapagos land iguana, *conolophus subcristatus,* on Santa Cruz Island.
Page 74 A land iguana on Santa Cruz Island.
Page 75 *Top:* The rear view of the land iguana on Santa Cruz Island shows its shorter and rounder tail.
Bottom: Woodcut 'Amblyrynchus Demarlu' from *Merveilles de la Nature.*

Page 76 Land iguana in sessuvium on South Plazas Island.
Page 77 *Top:* Land iguana in habitat, Santa Cruz Island.
Center: Land iguana on Santa Cruz Island.
Bottom: Land iguana in opuntia forest.
Page 78 A land iguana enjoys a cactus lunch on South Plazas Island.
Page 79 Land iguanas on South Plazas Island *(top)* and Santa Cruz Island *(bottom).*
Page 80/81 The smaller and prettier Galapagos lava lizard, *tropiduris sp.,* on James Island.
Page 82 *Left:* A side view of the beautiful lava lizard, South Plazas Island.
Bottom right: The colorful head of the lava lizard as it lies in wait for its lunch, Jervis Island off James Island.
Page 83 *Top:* A scarlet-throated lava lizard on Jervis Island.
Bottom left: A lava lizard clings to a branch after a heavy

lunch, Hood Island.
Bottom right: A startled lava lizard on Fernandina Island.
Page 84 The slender tapering body and tail of the lava lizard on South Plazas Island.
Page 85 Small tree finch, *camarhynchus parvulus.*
Page 88/89 Large ground finch, *geospiza magnirostris,* on James Island.
Inset top page 88: Cactus finch, *geospiza scandens,* on South Plazas Island.
Inset bottom page 88: Large ground finch on James Island.
Inset page 89: Small ground finch, *geospiza fuliginoza,* on Hood Island.
Page 90/91 Medium ground finch, *geospiza fortis,* on South Plazas Island.
Page 92/93 A Galapagos sea-lion takes in the sun on James Island.
Page 94/95 Two Galapagos fur seals, *arctocephalus australis galapagoensis,* 'talk' to each other on James Island.
Inset left page 94: Sea-lions try to find shade from the midday sun on Loberia Island.
Inset right page 94: Sea-lions on the sandy beach of Loberia Island.

Inset left page 95: A mother sea-lion and her pups on Loberia Island beach.
Inset right page 95: A family of sea-lions on the beach of Loberia Island.
Page 96/97 A sea-lion suns himself on a rock on Hood Island.
Page 98 A sea-lion enjoys a leisurely swim off Fernandina Island.
Page 99 *Top:* A sea-lion and her pup enjoy the foam on South Plazas Island.
Bottom: The lava rocks afford some shade for a sea-lion on Fernandina Island.
Page 100 *Top left:* A lonely fur seal pup on James Island.
Top right: Fur seals on the rocks of James Island.
Bottom left: A sleeping sea-lion with young on South Plazas Island.
Bottom right: Sea-lions on James Island.
Page 101 *Top left:* Sea-lions on Loberia Island.
Top right: A lost sea-lion pup among the smaller rocks on Loberia Island.
Bottom left: A sea-lion seeks shade under a bush on Loberia Island.
Bottom right: Sea-lions look seaward from James Island.

8

crowned night heron, *nyctanassa violacea*, in James Bay.
Top right: A yellow-crowned night heron on Isabela Island.
Below: A yellow-crowned night heron, James Bay.
Page 134/135 Red-billed tropic birds, *paethon aethereus*, in flight off South Plazas Island.
Inset page 134: Red-billed tropic birds on South Plazas Island.
Inset page 135: Red-billed tropic birds on Champion Island.
Page 136/137 Galapagos albatross, *diomeda irrorata*, in flight off Hood Island.
Bottom left: A pair of Galapagos albatrosses meet and the courting dance begins, Hood Island.
Bottom: First they bow…
Bottom right: and then they boast,
Page 138/139 *Top left:* followed by a kiss,
Top center: another bow,
Top right: another kiss.
Bottom left: The courting continues–

Bottom center: a kiss . . .
Bottom right: followed by an admiring look.
Page 140/141 *Top left:* One albatross scrutinizes the other . . .
Top center: before the dance continues with another kiss, and . . .
Top right: another bow.
Bottom left: The dance is also being watched.
Bottom center: The new admirer introduces himself . . .
Bottom right: and the exhausted loser walks away.
Page 142 The great frigate bird off Hood Island.
Page 143 *Top:* The great frigate bird, Hood Island.
Below: American oystercatcher, *haematopus palliatus*, on Hood Island.
Page 144/145 *(All three)* Swallow-tailed gulls on Champion Island.
Page 146 *(All three)* Swallow-tailed gulls on Champion Island.
Page 148/149 The brown pelican, *pelicanus occidentalis*, in

flight at sunset, Baltra Island.
Insets: Brown pelicans on the rocks of Baltra Island.
Page 150 *Top left:* A brown pelican waits for dinner on a rock offshore at James Bay.
Top right: A brown pelican takes flight, James Bay.
Bottom left: A pelican in flight with Fernandina Island in the background.
Bottom right: A brown pelican rests on Fernandina Island.
Page 151 A brown pelican in flight.
Page 152/153 The red-footed booby, *sula sula*.
Inset: Red-footed booby.
Page 154/155 Blue-footed booby, *sula nebouxii*, on Jervis Island.
Inset page 154: A back view of the blue-footed booby at the Daphne Crater.
Inset page 155: A frontal portrait of the blue-footed booby on Champion Island.
Page 156 A blue-footed booby lands in some bushes on Champion Island.
Page 157 *(All four)* A pair of

blue-footed boobies imitates the courtship dance of the Galapagos albatrosses.
Page 158 *Top:* Blue-footed boobies on their nest on Champion Island.
Bottom: Blue-footed boobies on a nest with an egg, Champion Island.
Page 159 A blue-footed booby with its chick, Jervis Island.
Page 160/161 A masked booby, *sula dactylatra*, nests under a sparsely foliaged tree on the rim of the Daphne Crater.
Inset page 161: A masked booby with chick, Daphne Crater.
Page 162/163 A masked booby in flight with Hood Island in the background.
Page 164 Masked boobies rest on the rim of the Daphne Crater.
Page 165 *Top:* A masked booby with her chick on Daphne Island.
Center and below: A pair of masked boobies on Daphne Island.
Page 175 A Galapagos penguin.

Foreword
by Roger Lewin

Two days after Christmas in 1831 a small ten-gun brig sailed gently from her moorings in the harbor of Devonport in the south of England, a steady wind filling the canvas strung from her three masts. The ship's name was HMS *Beagle* and it was skippered by Captain Robert Fitzroy, an aristocrat (he was in fact an illegitimate descendant of King Charles II) who sported a powerful but irascible personality. Also on board was an apparently much less impressive character: a quiet, reticent young man in his early twenties, he was a Cambridge graduate in Theology, Euclid, and the Classics, and had a keen taste for natural history. This was Charles Darwin, the man who almost 30 years later was to initiate what is arguably the greatest revolution of all time concerning man's view of himself in relation to the world and to God.

During the long, gruelling, but unquestionably exhilarating, voyage that began at the end of that Christmas season of 1831, Darwin amassed huge amounts of information about rocks, animals, and plants that enabled him, in 1859, to publish the book for which he is most famous: *The Origin of Species*. It was this book that ignited the revolution, reverberations of which still echo in some scientific and religious establishments the world over.

What Darwin saw on the five-year voyage of the *Beagle* eventually convinced him that animals and plants are not the products of special creation as Victorian society believed. He realized that, instead, all living things – including humans – are part of a richly varied and dynamic state of change – a steady process of evolution. In other words, species of animals and plants are not fixed and unchangeable: over long periods of time they may adapt to new environments eventually to become new species. The realization that humans too are caught up in the continuous process of evolution – that man is *a part of* nature rather than being *apart from* it – was the nub of the intellectual readjustment forced by the Darwinian revolution. The suggestion that humans are not only related to the animal world but also that man is actually descended from a more primitive animal stock was repugnant to many people. Indeed, the notion flew audaciously in the face of religious teaching of the time. After a surprisingly brief but bitter intellectual struggle, however, Darwin's theory was largely accepted.

Darwin's journey on the *Beagle* had taken him right around the world, and it included stops at small islands and major continents in the southern hemisphere as Captain Fitzroy carried out the task of marine survey with which he had been charged by the British government. The young naturalist saw many sites to wonder at, both animate and inanimate. But of all the places he visited, the one of unchallenged importance was the Galapagos Islands, a cluster of more or less rugged volcanic cones that pierce the deep waters of the Pacific Ocean 600 miles west of Ecuador in South America. It was here that Darwin was most impressed with the adaptability of animal and plant species in their unusual island environment. It was here that the revolution expressed in *The Origin of Species* was conceived. And it is therefore the Galapagos Islands that now represent the scientific focus of the greatest intellectual – and emotional – revolution that man has ever faced.

Five major islands, plus a scattering of smaller islands and giant rocks, form the Gala-

A swallow-tailed gull, *creagus furcatus,* on South Plazas Island.

The *Beagle* and the *Adventure*
in the Straits of Magellan.
Painting by J W Carmichael.
National Maritime Museum,
Greenwich.

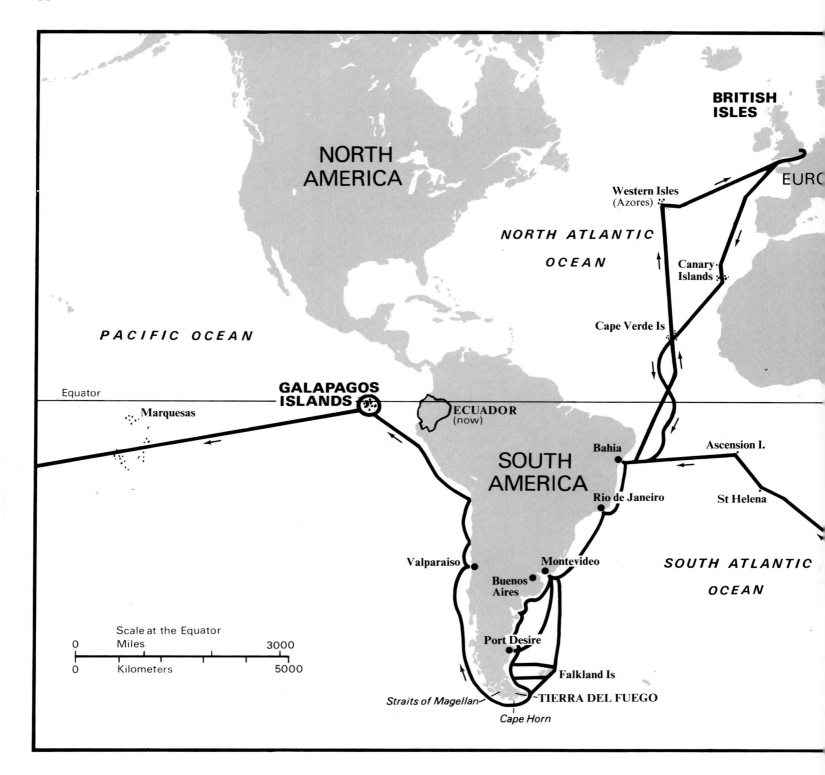

pagos Archipelago. They are the tips of gigantic volcanoes that thrust two miles through the Pacific waters before breaking surface astride the equator. One of them, Fernandina, climbs upwards for another mile, ending in a magnificent cone that is often draped in mist. Mist is a frequent companion of the islands; a soft, silent, enveloping sheet from which the stark rock may suddenly appear, only to vanish from sight again just as unexpectedly. It was this unnerving quality of unreality, plus the insistent calms that frequently hold the area in an expectant breathless state, that led early sailors to call the archipelago *Las Islas Encantadas,* the Enchanted Isles.

When, in the seventeenth century, English adventurers set sail in search of the islands they were taunted by Spaniards who said that what they sought were enchanted lands, 'shadows and noe reall Islands.' Even though the islands *are* real, they are no less enchanting for that: they set a stage of harsh grey and black volcanic rock patterned here and there by rope-like whirls of cooled larva; festoons of lichen splash green and brown

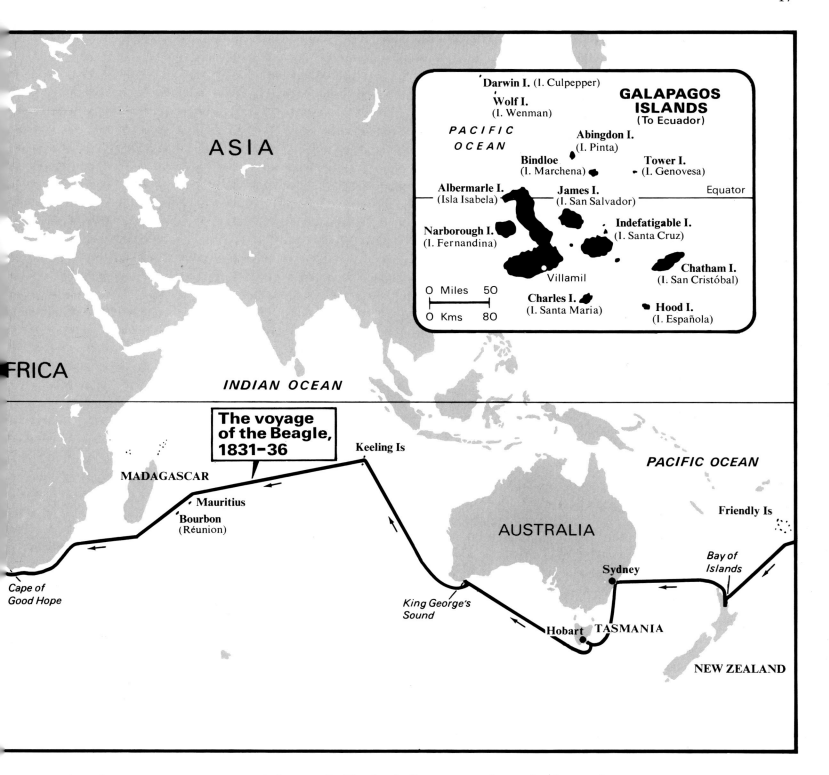

The voyage
of the Beagle,
1831-36

GALAPAGOS
ISLANDS
(To Ecuador)

PACIFIC OCEAN

Darwin I. (I. Culpepper)

Wolf I.
(I. Wenman)

Abingdon I.
(I. Pinta)

Bindloe
(I. Marchena)

Tower I.
(I. Genovesa)

Albermarle I.
(Isla Isabela)

James I.
(I. San Salvador)

Equator

Narborough I.
(I. Fernandina)

Indefatigable I.
(I. Santa Cruz)

Chatham I.
(I. San Cristóbal)

Villamil

Charles I.
(I. Santa Maria)

Hood I.
(I. Española)

O Miles 50

O Kms 80

ASIA

AFRICA

INDIAN OCEAN

Keeling Is

MADAGASCAR

Mauritius

Bourbon
(Réunion)

AUSTRALIA

PACIFIC OCEAN

Friendly Is

Sydney

Bay of Islands

Cape of
Good Hope

King George's
Sound

Hobart   TASMANIA

NEW ZEALAND

against the grey; mangrove trees balance stilt-like in shallow water; huge slender cacti stab the warm air; the arid lowlands give way to lush forest on the hill slopes; but nothing, save for a greyish-white lichen, grows near the lips of the volcanoes as they gape round-mouthed to the skies. There is movement too as strange dragon-like lizards shift on the coarse rock, their scaly bodies basking in the hot sun, enormous tortoises lumber lazily in search of fresh water, sealions squabble crossly on the beach, and birds large and small pierce the air both with their calls and their quick flight.

The Galapagos is a place of breath-taking contrasts: parched desert stands in sight of cool lush forest; the dull, almost threatening, grey of the volcanic rock is mercifully relieved by soft greens and browns of persistent plants and by the constantly moving web of color woven by the nervously darting brilliant red Sally Lightfoot crabs; and there is the ever-present sound of the sea as it slowly but inexorably works the rock into sand. Dominated as they are by large impressive reptiles, the Galapagos Islands are biologically

18

Far left: Vice-Admiral Robert FitzRoy.
Left: Charles Darwin as a young man.
Below: The *Beagle* in Murray Narrow—Beagle Channel. Painting by Conrad Mortens, Down House, Kent.

unique in the world. Indeed, so unfamiliar is the animal cast on the islands' stage that one has the uneasy feeling of having blundered back through time to a previous age when mammals played an insignificant role in life's drama.

It was upon this strange world that Fray Tomás de Berlanga, fourth Bishop of Panama, stumbled unwittingly early in 1535. Following the orders of the Spanish Emperor Charles V, the Bishop set sail from Panama for Peru to report on conditions there following political strife. 'The ship sailed with very good breezes for seven days,' the Bishop wrote to the Emperor but then ill-fortune struck in the form of 'a six-day calm.' The Bishop went on to explain that 'the currents were so strong and engulfed us in such a way that on Wednesday, 10 March, we sighted an island.'

The ship had been swept westwards by the powerful Humbolt current that for much of the year bathes the Galapagos Islands in cool waters from near the Antarctic. Running short of fresh water and food the sailors accompanying the Bishop were ecstatic, albeit somewhat nervous, at the prospect of replenishing their stores: 'they agreed to lower the life-boat and go on land for water and grass for the horses.' Once on dry land, however, they found no water: they saw 'nothing but seals, and turtles, and such big tortoises, that each could carry a man on top of itself, and many iguanas that are like serpents.'

Disappointed with the results of their first foray, the sailors moved to another island. 'On this second one,' the Bishop related to the Emperor, 'the same conditions prevailed as on the first; many seals, turtles, iguanas, tortoises, many birds like those of Spain but so silly that they do not know how to flee and many were caught in the hand.' Faced with the harsh volcanic scenery the Bishop said of the island, 'I do not think that there is a place where one might sow a bushel of corn, because most of it is full of very big stones, so much so, that it seems as though some time God had showered stones . . .' Eventually the Bishop and his crew did find water, and, after taking on board what he thought would be sufficient to supply them during their journey, they set sail for the mainland. Eventually

Map of the Galapagos Archipelago taken from Darwin's 'The Voyage of the *Beagle.*'

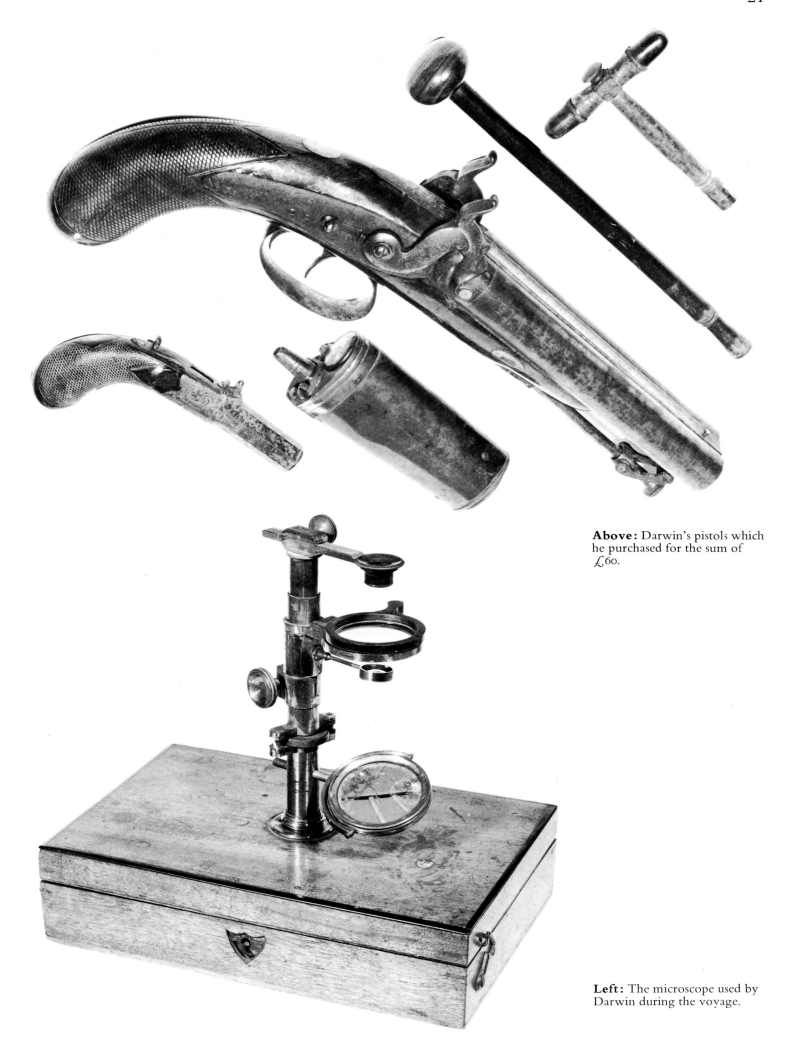

Above: Darwin's pistols which he purchased for the sum of £60.

Left: The microscope used by Darwin during the voyage.

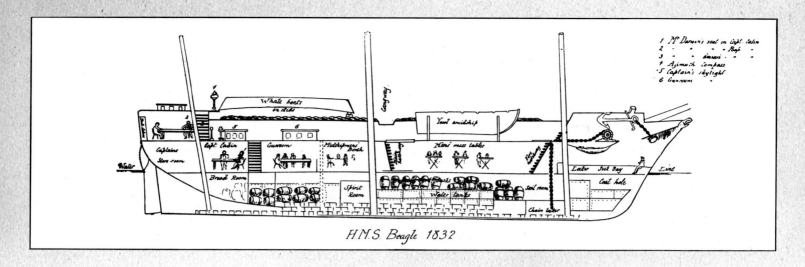

H.M.S. Beagle 1832

Left: A plan of the *Beagle* showing the side-elevation. **Below:** Male and female vermillion flycatchers, *pyrocephalus rubinus*.

they arrived safely (but not before they had run through all their water rations and had been forced instead to drink wine!) and were able to report the discovery of the new islands. This was almost exactly 300 years before HMS *Beagle* sailed into the same treacherous waters.

Since Tomás de Berlanga drifted into sight of the first of the Galapagos Islands (it was probably Santa Fé) whilst in the unyielding grip of the Humbolt current, the archipelago has been discovered and rediscovered many times. As a result each island has been blessed with many names: most have had as many as five names, and one boasts eight! But, because of their extreme isolation in their far flung part of the Pacific, and also because they are for the most part inhospitable, the Galapagos Islands have led a relatively quiet – though colorful – history. During the sixteenth century, for instance, the vessels of Spanish adventurers were to be seen among the islands. Later, British buccaneers pursuing their trade of piracy and plundering along the Spanish-American coast exploited the islands' obscurity as a safe place from which to pounce.

Fresh water and food in plentiful supply and in such an out of the way spot made the pirates' business so much easier than it might otherwise have been. Judging from the litter of glass and pottery they left behind there, James Bay and Buccaneer Bay on the Island of Santiago were well used by the pirates. Level open ground with the pleasant shade of a few scattered trees offered a place in which to relax between the serious business of plundering passing ships!

With piracy on the wane during the eighteenth century, the rise of the Pacific whaling industry brought a new phase of life to the Enchanted Isles. British and New England whalers used the islands as a source of water and fresh food, tortoises being particularly favored because they remained alive for a long time on board without food or water: their meat therefore stayed fresh. Some of the largest ships would load up to 800 of these prehistoric giants at any one time, a practice that began the steady and virtually catastrophic decline in their numbers. The Galapagos Islands became more and more popular

as a port of call for whalers right through until the late nineteenth century. At the beginning of the nineteenth century the agents of the fur seal industry continued the gory plunder.

The Galapagos Archipelago is probably the most active set of volcanic islands in the world, a feature that cannot have escaped the attention of its many visitors during the centuries since its discovery. One vessel, the *Tartar,* almost perished during a spectacular eruption of Fernandina in 1825 The *Tartar,* under Captain Benjamin Morrell, had come to the islands on a sealing expedition, and, on the night of 14 February, it was lying quietly at anchor after a successful – and bloody – day of carnage on the beaches. 'While the sable mantle of night was yet spread over the mighty Pacific, shrouding the neighboring islands from our view,' wrote Morrell in his diary,' and while the stillness of death reigned everywhere about us, our ears were suddenly assailed by a sound that could only be equaled by 10,000 thunders bursting upon the air at once; while at the same instant, the whole hemisphere was lighted up with a horrid glare that might have appalled the stoutest heart!' 'Fernandina, the most westerly of all the islands, exploded and began pouring molten larva down its rugged slopes and belching smoke, ash, and flame into the night sky.

'Had it been the "crack of doom" that aroused them, my men could not have been sooner on deck, where they stood gazing like sheeted specters, speechless and bewildered with astonishment and dismay,' Morrell recorded. 'The heavens appeared to be one blaze of fire, intermingled with millions of falling stars and meteors.' Truly, it must have been a wondrous sight. But the sailors' sense of awe soon turned to concern for their lives as they realized that they must sail out of danger. But, as luck would have it, the *Tartar's* canvasses hung listless in one of the calms for which the islands are famous – or rather infamous. The Captain and his men could only pray for wind as they felt the ever-rising heat on their faces and heard the boiling of the sea as molten larva hit the cold waters: 'The demon of fire seemed rushing to the embraces of Neptune; and dreadful indeed was

The *Beagle* in the Straits of Magellan with Mount Sarmiento in the distance. Print from 'The Voyage of the *Beagle.*'

the uproar occasioned by their meeting. The ocean boiled and roared and bellowed, as if a civil war had broken out in the Tartarean gulf.'

Eventually a breeze blew up and Captain Morrell was able to steer his ship to safety but not before melted pitch had begun running from the ship's seams and rigging. The temperature on deck at one point was 147°F! The stark landscape of many of the Galapagos Islands has inspired more than one visitor to compare them to some part of hell. The night of 14 February 1825 must have seemed closer than was comfortable to that undesirable place.

Just over ten years after Captain Morrell and his terrified crew escaped narrowly with their lives on that February night, HMS *Beagle* dropped anchor off the shore of San Cristobal: the date was 17 September 1835. This was the beginning of the *Beagle's* five week sojourn among the Galapagos Islands, a visit that was destined to sow important seeds in Charles Darwin's mind about the nature of life and creation.

Charles Island clearly showing the volcanic peak of the Island. Print from 'The Voyage of the *Beagle.*'

Hood Island

Darwin, born on 12 February 1809 (the same day as Abraham Lincoln), was the second son of Robert Waring Darwin, a prosperous doctor in Shrewsbury, a small town in south-west England. Standing more than six feet tall and weighing 24 stone, Robert Darwin was in his son Charles' eyes, 'the largest man who I ever saw.' Charles also considered his father to be 'the kindest man I ever knew.' In spite of his alleged kindness, Robert Darwin inspired in his son a respect that bordered on terror. Robert Darwin was a deeply devout man, a factor that may explain why Charles was apparently so reluctant to publish his theory of evolution as it challenged all that his formidable father stood for. Charles' mother, who died when he was eight, was the daughter of Josiah Wedgwood, a member of the famous English pot makers.

At the age of 16 Darwin, following his father's wishes, went to Edinburgh University to read medicine, a topic for which he had little enthusiasm. His fragile interest in medicine collapsed completely when he saw an operation performed without anaesthetic – in fact,

he absented himself from the operating theater with undignified haste before the surgery was completed! During two years at Edinburgh, Darwin learned little to do with medicine but he was able to pursue his interest in natural history; he also learned how to stuff birds and animals, a skill that was to be invaluable during his scientific odyssey on the *Beagle*.

Lava flow on James Island.

Acknowledging that his son would never become a medical man, Robert Darwin then sent Charles to Cambridge where he was to be instructed in Theology as preparation for going into the Church. Robert Darwin was, apparently, somewhat concerned that Charles should not turn into 'an idle sporting man' – Charles had a passion for shooting, a sport that, in his father's opinion, encouraged him to mix in undesirable company.

At Cambridge, as at Edinburgh, Charles was not particularly committed to his formal studies. Instead, he preferred to develop his interests in botany and geology, in which he was encouraged by Professors John Henslow and Adam Sedgwick. These two men, who were respectively Professors of Botany and Geology at the University, had a great influence on the young Darwin's future career.

Darwin left Cambridge in the Spring of 1831 with a not unreasonable degree in Theology but certainly with no ambition to become a clergyman. His father was not pleased. In August that year Henslow wrote to Darwin telling him of an offer made by a Captain Fitzroy: the Captain was prepared 'to give up part of his own cabin to any young man who would volunteer to go with him without pay as a naturalist to the voyage of the *Beagle*'. Henslow considered Darwin to be suitable for the position. Charles was keen to take up the offer. But Robert Darwin forbade him to go. However, Charles' father was prevailed upon by Josiah Wedgwood, and eventually permission was granted. Wedgwood was anxious that Charles should take the opportunity because he saw his nephew as 'a man of enlarged curiosity.' With this enlarged curiosity—and the ability to stuff birds—as virtually his only qualification for the job, Charles set out on his momentous voyage. He was seasick constantly for the first two weeks!

The intellectual world in which Darwin was educated was rigorously structured by the church's teachings. In spite of mounting geological evidence to the contrary, many people still considered the earth to be a mere 6000 years old, a figure that derived from a statement made in 1650 by James Ussher, Archbishop of Armagh. And all animals and plants were said to be the products of divine creation. Indeed, if the earth really was so very young there would have been insufficient time for a more gradual progressive evolution to have taken place. The layers of fossils of extinct animals showing increasing complexity as time passed was explained as the result of successive creations following catastrophies such as the Noachim flood (someone calculated that there had been 31 creations in all). Species of animals and plants were therefore viewed as fixed, unchangeable, immutable organisms in a very young world. The idea that living things might adapt to their surroundings through long periods of time was simply not countenanced by the greater part of the scientific establishment and certainly not by the religious establishment.

Left: Albemarle Island.

Not everyone accepted the line of argument supported by the church, however, and indeed one of the voices that had publicly entertained alternative suggestions was that of Erasmus Darwin, Charles' grandfather. But the problem faced by the growing band of pro-evolutionists was that they had no single coherent theory that they could enthusiastically champion as a group. For this they had to wait until 1859, the publication of *The Origin of Species*.

In order that the notion of gradual change through time – evolution – could be seriously promulgated, two things were needed: first, the earth must be shown to be considerably older than the 6000 years favored by the teachings of Ussher; second, it was necessary to have unquestionable evidence that living things can adapt to the opportunities offered by their environment, that they do evolve.

As Darwin set off on the *Beagle* in 1831 the first of these conditions was being satisfied by his great friend Sir Charles Lyell, the acknowledged leader of geology in Britain. He

Below: Devil's Crown off Floreana Island.

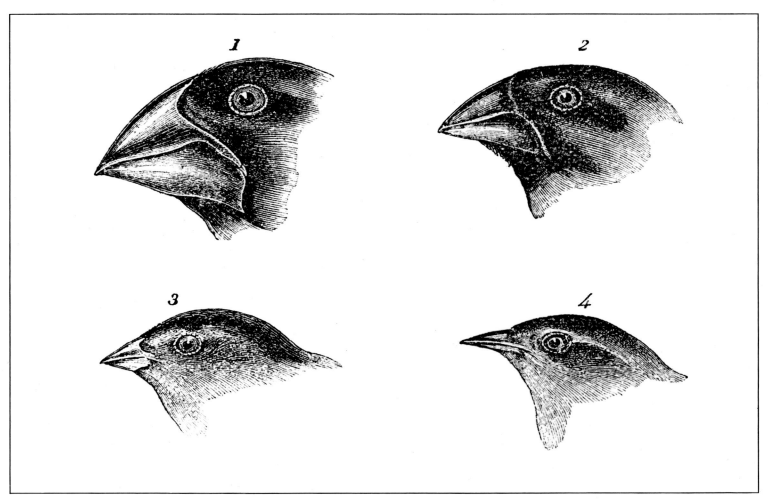

Above: The four graduations of beak sizes of the Galapagos finches.

had become convinced, and he was beginning successfully to convince others, that rocks are the product of very, very slow processes that go on for a very, very long time. The world simply had to be extremely ancient, thus providing a time frame within which evolution could have occurred.

The second of the two conditions – collecting the evidence of evolution – was what Darwin was about to achieve through his work on the *Beagle*, particularly in the Galapagos Islands. There was also of course the question of the *mechanism* by which evolution might operate. This was to occur to Darwin a little over a year after he returned in 1836 from his circumnavigation of the world in the *Beagle*.

During the first – but lengthy – part of its voyage the *Beagle* skirted the east and west coasts of the South American continent, making many stops including Bahia, Rio de Janeiro, Montevideo, Port Desire, the Falkland Islands, and Valparaiso on the way. While Captain Fitzroy charted the waters of ports thought to be important for the use of the British navy, Darwin spent his time collecting plants, animals, and insects, although he was principally interested in geology. It was an adventurous time for the young man, with political revolutions, long exhausting horseback rides, and life-threatening fever all featuring in his demanding routine. When, in September 1835, the *Beagle* turned her bow towards the open Pacific Darwin was feeling well pleased with his previous three years accomplishments around South America. He did not know that the five weeks he was to spend among the Enchanted Isles were destined to shift his interest from geology to biology and were to provide him with the vital clues to the question of the fixity of species.

Darwin was immediately struck by the vistas of volcanism presented by the Galapagos Islands. In his journal of the voyage of the *Beagle* he recorded that the islands 'are all formed of volcanic rocks . . . Some of the craters, surmounting the larger islands, are of immense size, and they rise to a height of between 3–5000 feet. Their flanks are studded with innumerable smaller orifaces. I scarcely hesitate to affirm, that there must be in the whole archipelago at least 2000 craters.' On the morning of 17 September the ship dropped

Left: A Galapagos finch.

anchor off San Cristobal. Clearly a little taken aback by what he saw, Darwin wrote in his journal that, 'Nothing could be less inviting than the first appearance. A broken field of black basaltic lava, thrown into the most rugged waves, and crossed by great fissures, is everywhere covered by stunted, sunburnt brushwood, which shows little signs of life.'

As if appearance were not bad enough, the rewards of collecting seemed frustratingly unpromising too: 'Although I diligently tried to collect as many plants as possible, I succeeded in getting very few; and such wretched-looking little weeds would have better become an arctic than an equatorial flora.' The *Beagle* put in at a number of points around San Cristobal, and as Darwin saw more and more of the island he gradually fell under its spell. Recording the stifling heat and fatigue of stumbling over the rough surface and through tangled thicket, he nevertheless was forced to admit that he 'was well repaid by the strange Cyclopean scene.' He wondered at the immense size of the tortoises and was amazed – as visitors still are today – by the extreme tameness of the animals and birds.

As Darwin became better acquainted with life on the Galapagos Archipelago he was more and more intrigued by what he saw. 'The natural history of these islands is eminently curious,' he wrote. He noted that most of the plants, animals, and birds living there were quite special to the islands, and yet they bore an unmistakeable resemblance to similar species on the mainland. More than that, each island had a selection of species characteristic of itself and quite unlike neighboring islands. 'The archipelago,' Darwin says, 'is a little world within itself.' Refering to the similarities with species on the mainland, he continues, saying 'or rather it is a satellite attached to America, whence it has derived a few stray colonists.'

Darwin recognized that the nature of the volcanic activity implied that the islands were geologically young (they are in fact just a few million years old). Inevitably, therefore, he was forced to contemplate how the islands had become populated so quickly with forms of life that, though special to the archipelago, carried an uncanny shadow of life elsewhere. All he could record in his journal at the time was his sense that he was seeing something important, the nature of which he was unclear about: 'we seem to be brought somewhat near to that great fact – that mystery of mysteries – the first appearance of new being on this earth.' It was to be some time before he understood that the evidence he was contemplating implied that species could change, that they are not the fixed products of creation. But he had begun to question.

The discovery that more than any other nudged Darwin's imagination in the direction of evolution of species was what he described as 'a most singular group of finches.' Thirteen species in all, they were clearly related to each other in the form of their body, plumage, and song. Yet they made their livings in very different ways: some cracked open hard nuts, others fed on soft fruit, while others lived on insects – one of them, called the woodpecker finch, actually fashions and uses a cactus spine with which it prizes insects from cracks in trees, just as a woodpecker does with its naturally elongated beak. The beaks of the Galapagos finches are formed according to the job they do: stocky and powerful in the nut-eaters; less robust in the fruit-eaters; and slender in those that live in insects.

Here, therefore, is a group of birds all undoubtedly related to each other, and related to a South American finch, and yet their beaks are perfectly adapted to their different ways of making a living. They appeared to be drawn from a single ancestor but they are distinctly different. How could this be? Darwin came close to the expression of adaptation to the environment by a process of slow evolution when he wrote in his journal: 'Seeing this gradation and diversity of structure in one small, intimately related group of birds, one might really fancy that from an original paucity of birds in this achipelago, one species had been taken and modified for different ends.'

It is not just the finches that display a spectrum of the apparent forces of creation. Tortoises, land iguanas, other birds, and plants vary from island to island too. Darwin was greatly impressed by the fact that each island had a more or less characteristic selection of species of animals and plants that, as a group, lived throughout the archipelago: he said that it is 'by far the most remarkable feature in the natural history.' Noting that most of the islands are within sight of each other, he wrote, 'that several of the islands possess their own species of tortoise, mocking-thrush, finches, and numerous plants, these species having the same general habits, occupying analagous situations, and obviously filling the same place in the natural economy of this archipelago, strikes me with wonder.'

By way of explanation of this striking diversity, Darwin points out that although the islands are close to each other they are separated by very deep water in which currents move very fast. It would therefore be very difficult for creatures to journey from island to island. Moreover, the lack of strong winds around the islands would also not favor the transport of small birds, insects, and light seeds between them. When he was concluding his initial notes on the archipelago, noting the effective isolation of each island from its neighbors, Darwin says that 'one is astonished at the amount of creative force, if such an expression may be used, displayed on these small, barren, and rocky islands.'

Darwin left the islands with great regret after his five-week exploration. He had memories of riding on giant tortoises, of clambering to the rims of countless volcanic cones, of examining the behavior of the only marine lizard in the world (the marine iguana), and of the remarkable tameness of the birds. But he also carried with him seeds of ideas about the nature of that 'creative force,' seeds that had been sown in a fertile mind.

On 2 October 1836 HMS *Beagle* dropped anchor at Falmouth, a small harbor in the south of England. After leaving the Galapagos Islands at the end of October 1835, Captain Fitzroy had steered his craft west across the Pacific to New Zealand. From there he, his crew and the now weary, but increasingly satisfied, unpaid naturalist visited Australia, some Indian Ocean islands, rounded the Cape of Good Hope, revisited Bahia in South America, and then returned north to home. Darwin was not unaffected by the inevitable privations of such a voyage and he said that 'the pleasures gained at the time do not counterbalance the evils. It is necessary to look forward to a harvest, however distant that may be, when some fruit will be reaped, to good effect.' Darwin's harvest was to be an unassailable volume of evidence that protected his highly controversial

The manuscript of Darwin's journal of 'The Voyage of the *Beagle*.'

theory on the origin of species. In 1836 the task that lay before him was that of analyzing and ordering the evidence collected on his epic scientific odyssey.

For whatever reason Darwin was apparently very reluctant to 'go public' with his ideas on evolution: perhaps he was supremely cautious lest his scientific reputation be put at risk; or maybe the inescapable emotional trauma was just too much for him to face. In any case, he first opened his notebook on what he called 'The Transmutation of Species' in July 1837 and it was not until 22 years later, 24 November 1859, that he published *The Origin of Species*. Moreover, Darwin would not have gone into print even at that late date had he not been forced into doing so by a short communication from another naturalist, Alfred Russel Wallace, which described a theory that was identical to Darwin's. (In 1858 Darwin and Wallace delivered a joint paper on the origin of species to the Linnaean Society in London, a major scientific event that passed entirely unnoticed.)

By the end of the voyage on the *Beagle* Darwin had begun to suspect that species are not immutable, that they may change and adapt to environmental opportunities that present themselves. Later, when back in England he started the arduous task of sifting through his vast collections, he became convinced of it. There remained the problem of *how* species changed – what mechanism operates? It was a little over a year after starting his notebook on 'The Transmutation of Species' that Darwin got the inspiration he sought. He had been reading an essay by Thomas Malthus on population when he suddenly saw his answer – natural selection.

Darwin knew that the products of sexual reproduction are not identical to the parents or to each other: the offspring vary and this to some degree is under genetic control. He realized that, because of certain subtle characteristics, one offspring may be better able to exploit a certain environment than his siblings. This individual may therefore be favored – just slightly – in the struggle for life and may therefore produce more than the average number of offspring in his turn. In this way the genetic characteristics of this individual would become more common in the population, and in the end (over a very

The new study of Down House, Kent Darwin's home.

Exterior of Down House, Kent, England.

long time and with sufficient selection pressure) a new species may emerge, related to the original one of course but clearly distinct from it. The emergence of new species in this way is particularly likely if groups of animals are geographically isolated from each other, a situation that is exemplified by the Galapagos Islands.

Darwin called this mechanism 'natural selection,' and as a concept it remains the basis of evolutionary thought right through into modern biology. Indeed the full title of his famous book is *The Origin of Species by Means of Natural Selection.* He also added a subtitle: *The Preservation of Favored Races in the Struggle for Life.* Although Darwin was completely aware of the implications for human origins that were embodied in his theory, he allowed himself just one ultra-low key reference to them in his book: he said that 'light will be thrown on the origin of man and his history.' In spite of his precaution Darwin's reading public settled almost exclusively on this single issue. It was inevitable.

The question of how life began on the Galapagos Islands is something of a mystery, or at least it is a matter of speculation. A few million years ago, at the time when the island first burst through the Pacific waters, the islands would have been not only lifeless but totally uninhabitable: boiling lava and noxious gases would have made it inaccessible to even the hardiest form of life. When the molten rock cooled and hardened and the gases dispersed, life became possible. What then was the source of the first colonists? Owing to the close identity of many Galapagos species with animals and plants in South America we can say securely that it was this continent that first breathed life into the sterile lands of the bleak cluster of volcanic cones 600 miles out into the Pacific. How?

Almost certainly the first colonists arrived by boat, or rather a natural raft of natural vegetation on which a selection of animals had unwittingly set sail. Today during the rainy seasons the swollen rivers of South America carry huge matted masses of trees, bushes, grass and other vegetation out into the ocean. Such rafting must have happened countless times in the past before one reached the shores of one of the virgin Galapagos Islands. Even then the passengers on the raft could not have survived in their new home unless spores and seeds of lichen, grasses, and bushes had been carried by strong winds long before to establish vegetation on which the newcomers could feed.

Once on the islands the animals were free to exploit the environment in any way they were able: as there was no indigenous population of creatures they were not constrained by any competition. Some of the iguanas remained firmly terrestrial, for instance, feeding on cactus and grasses, while others took the unusual step of returning to the sea. Some tortoises settled in the relative affluence of lush vegetation and developed domed shells, whereas others made a living in more arid areas where they evolved saddleback shells which allow them greater access to food hung high in bushes. In the absence of serious predators, the cormorant retained its fine ability to swim in search of fish but lost its ability to fly. The finches in their drab colored coats (the males are black and the females brown) took advantage of the minimum competition from other birds and started to make a living in many different ways: eventually, instead of there being just one species of finch as there probably was originally, there emerged 13, each physically adapted to live in a particular way. The isolation of the archipelago from the mainland, and the relative isolation of each island from its neighbors, permitted a unique field experiment in the dynamics of evolution.

Even when Darwin chanced upon this truly wonderful biological phenomenon a century and a half ago, man had already begun to inflict change in a way that only the human hand is capable of. Principal among this was the inexorable destruction for meat and for profit of the tortoise, an atavistic giant that had lumbered unwittingly into a modern world. When the islands were first discovered these enormous animals lived in countless thousands. According to one early visitor, it was possible to move about the Island of Isabela by stepping from one of these giants to another.

Although this undoubtedly is the exaggeration of an explorer anxious to impress his friends back home with wonderful tales, it does give some indication of the change between then and now: the tortoises of the Galapagos are now considered rare, there being perhaps 6000 in the whole archipelago. And of the 15 races of tortoises that once existed, four have slid into extinction, lost forever. A further race on Fernandina looks destined for extinction, there being only one known surviving individual. On Española until recently there were a mere 15 individuals who spent so much of their time wandering around the large arid island in search of rapidly vanishing food supplies that they rarely, if ever, met for mating. Although the situation on some other islands is less acute, overall the plight of the Galapagos tortoises is unquestionably serious.

The principal threat to the biology of Darwin's lost world is of course man, directly and indirectly. First, settlers on the islands, and visitors to them, inevitably encroach on the natural environment. The population of settlers is now around 5000 who live mainly on San Cristobal, Santa Cruz, and Isabela, with a small number on Floreana. The Ecuadorian government, whose province the archipelago is, has now declared nine-tenths of the lands as national park and it intends to keep the population at its present level. Tourism among the islands is becoming increasingly popular, and from a mere handful of visitors at the beginning of the 1970s the annual figure is now touching 10,000. Once again the Ecuadorian government is taking measures to control this activity and it is imposing a maximum of 12,000 visitors each year. Development of the settlers' lands and of facilities for tourists is inevitable and desirable but it must be done with a keen sense of conservation if the islands are to retain any semblance of the biological phenomenon they once were.

The biggest threat to the islands, however, is not the humans themselves but the animals they have introduced: goats, dogs, cats, black rats, pigs, and donkeys run wild on many of the islands and are wreaking havoc. Previously the home almost exclusively of reptiles, the Galapagos Islands are extremely vulnerable to the greater efficiency of mammals. The introduced goats and their other feral companions therefore thrive unchallenged. Many islands have been devastated by these invasions, vegetation and the young and eggs of lizards, birds and tortoises being consumed with unbridled enthusiasm. The loss of vegetation means more than a lost food supply for the indigenous animals: it rapidly invites the specter of severe soil erosion from which the islands can never recover. With the support of an increasingly oil-rich Ecuador, and international agencies such as UNESCO, and The International Union for the Conservation of Nature, this menace is beginning to be tackled by scientists at the research station of the Charles Darwin Foundation situated on Santa Cruz.

The personnel at the station not only carry out basic research on the unusual ecosystems of the islands (more than 500 international scientists have now visited the station) but, often with the aid of grants from the World Wildlife Fund, they attempt either to control or even exterminate the pests. Moreover, the station now has a nursery for breeding the endangered tortoises, a venture that is proving extremely successful and is turning out to be a great tourist attraction. The fundamental research is vital, however, if the complex interactions of animals and plants in the islands is to be properly understood. With this knowledge, sensitive conservation can be planned rationally.

Once the immediate peril of feral animals is dealt with, the long term future of the

Charles Darwin as an old man.

Galapagos Islands depends on a balance between the pressures for extreme conservation on the one hand and the countervailing forces of development and tourism on the other. If Darwin were to see the Enchanted Isles now he would undoubtedly be shocked at the devastation that has ripped through many of the islands and that threatens to engulf others. Unless the different and conflicting demands on the biology of the archipelago can be sensitively and constructively resolved, Darwin's forgotten world will be lost forever.

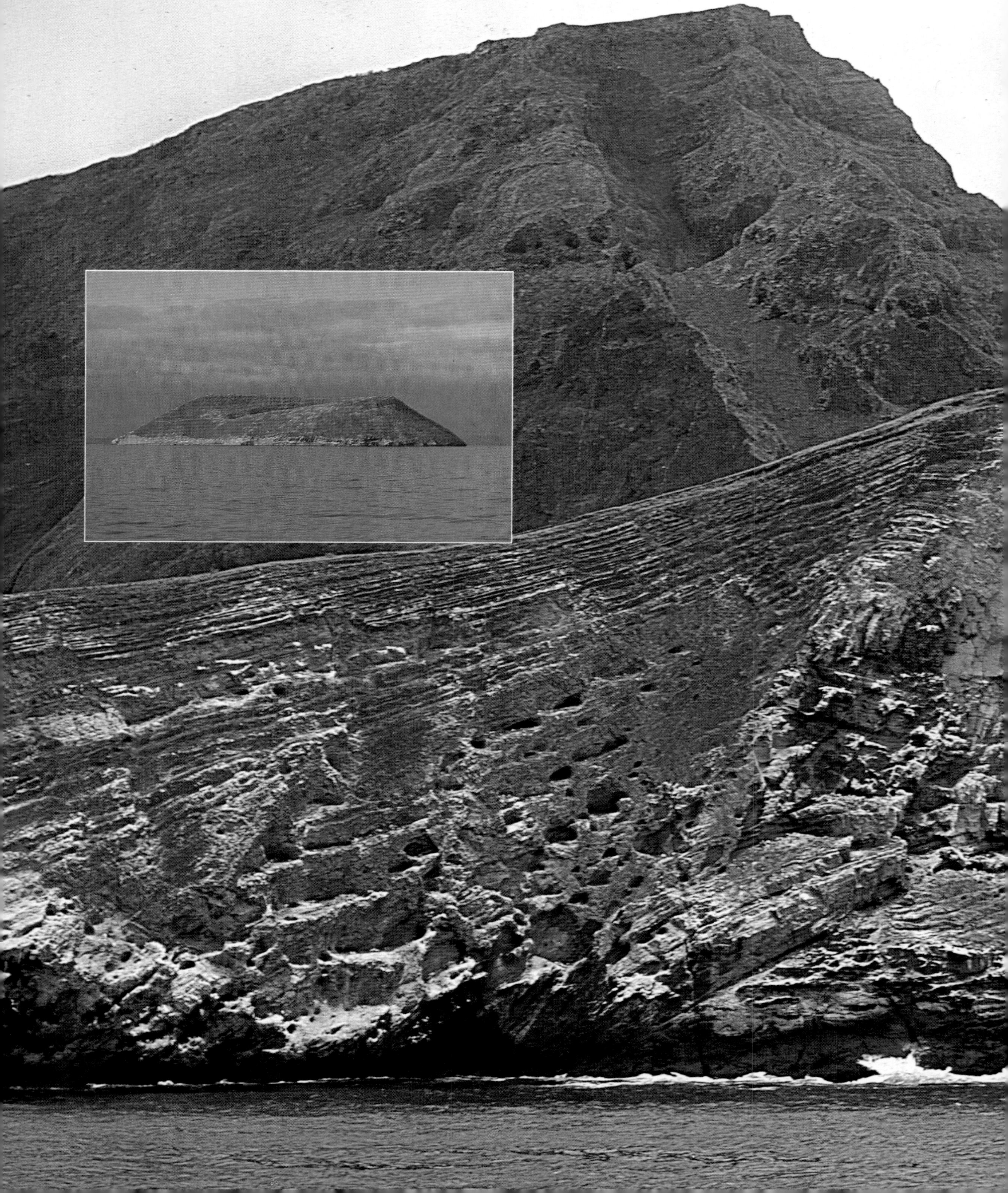

The Galapagos Archipelago

'This archipelago consists of ten principal islands, of which five exceed the others in size. They are situated under the Equator, and between five and six hundred miles westward of the coast of America.'

'They are all formed of volcanic rocks'.

'Some of the craters, surmounting
the larger islands, are of immense
size, and they rise to a height of
between three and four thousand
feet.'

'Nothing could be less inviting
than the first appearance.
A broken field of black basaltic
lava, thrown into the most rugged
waves, and crossed by great
fissures, is every where covered
by stunted, sun-burnt brushwood,
which shows little signs of life.'

'The commonest bush is one of the Euphorbiaceæ: an acacia and a great odd-looking cactus are the only trees which afford any shade.'

Galapagos Tortoises

'The old males are the largest'.

'One was eating
a piece of cactus.'

'The tortoise is very fond of water,
drinking large quantities,
and wallowing in the mud'.

'They frequent in preference the high damp parts.'

'Some grow to an immense size ... so large, that it required six or eight men to lift them from the ground.'

Marine Iguanas

'The rocks on the coast abounded
with great black lizards.'

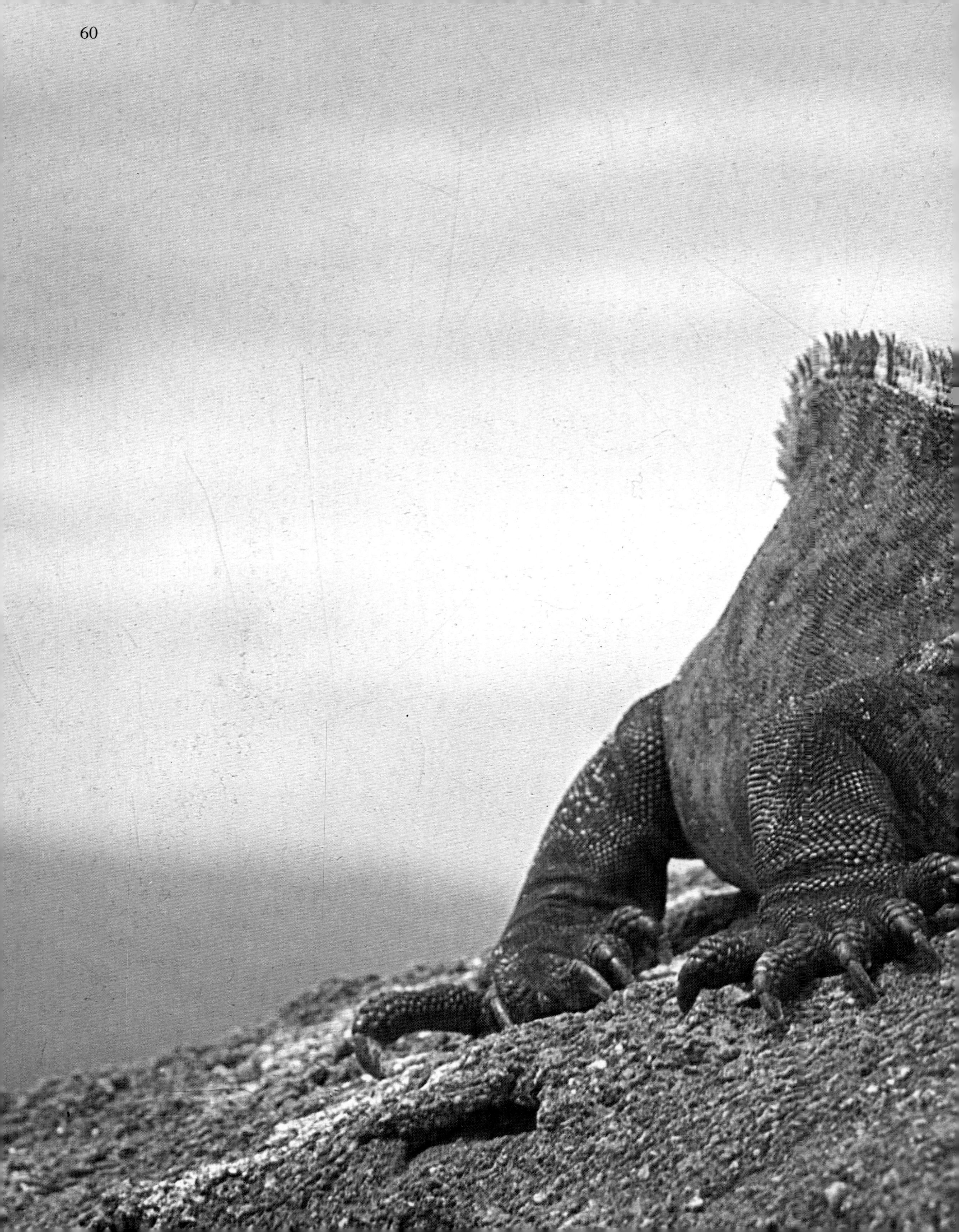

'Short, broad head,
and strong claws.'

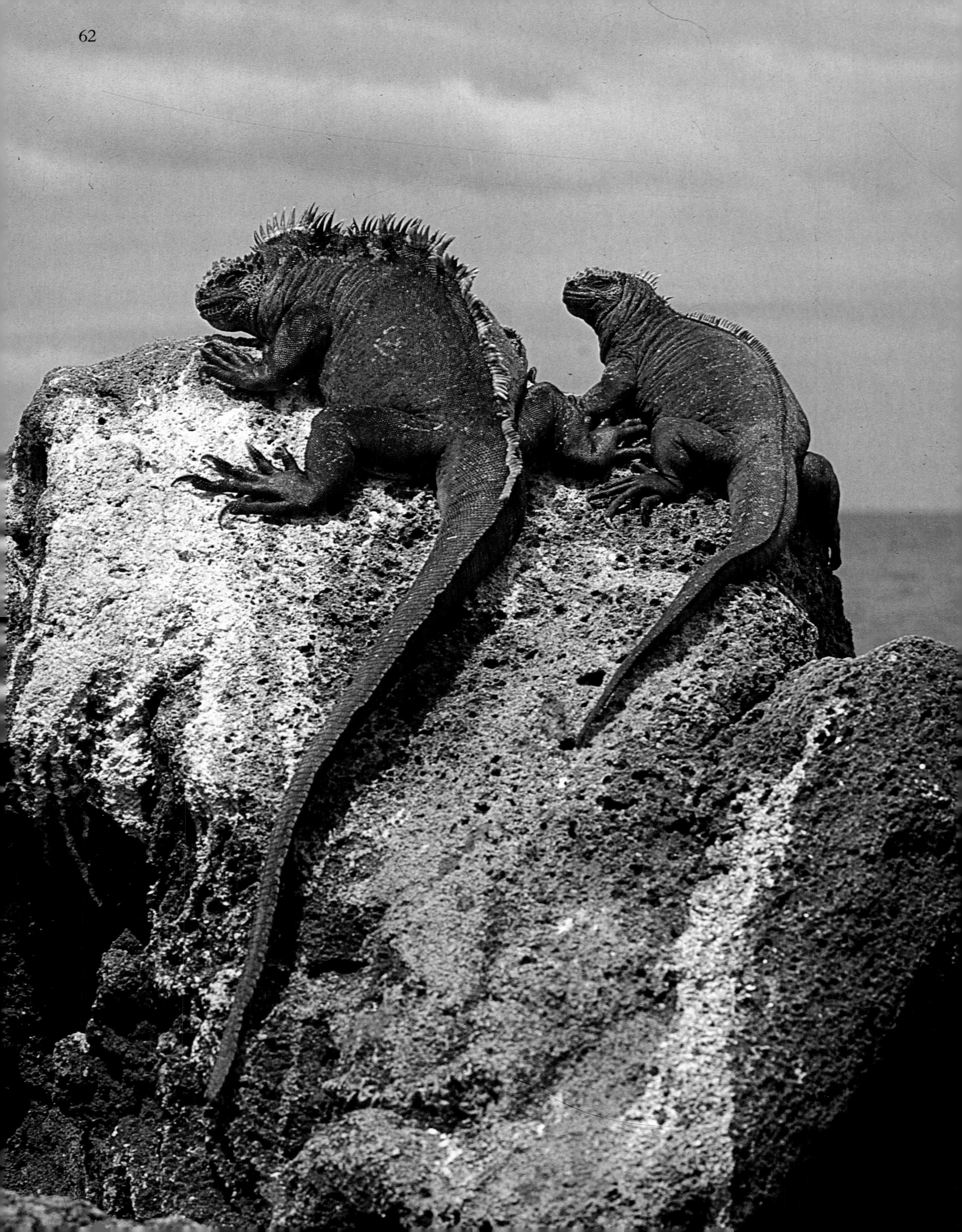

'It is a hideous-looking creature,
of a dirty black colour.'

'The usual length of a full-grown
one is about a yard, but there
are some even four feet long.'

'Quite stupid and sluggish
in it's movements.'

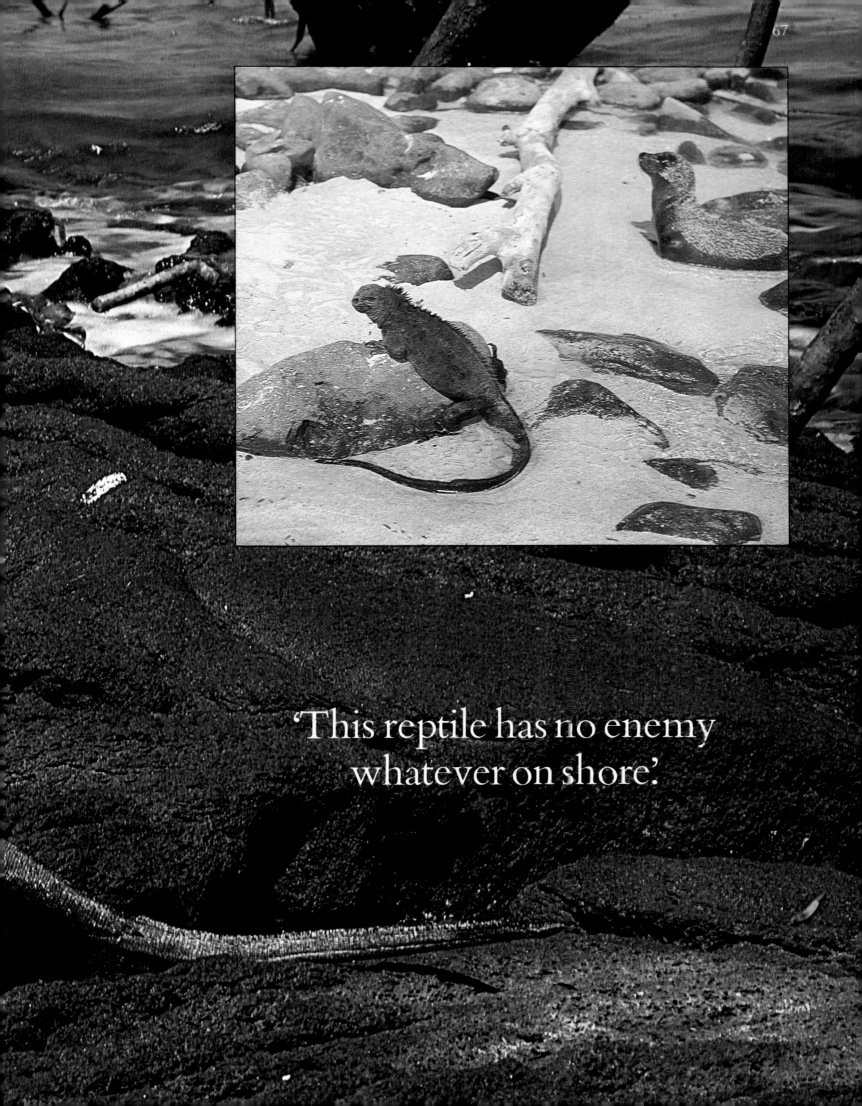

'This reptile has no enemy
whatever on shore.'

'Their limbs and strong claws are admirably adapted for crawling over the rugged and fissured masses of lava.'

'Oftentimes be seen on the black rocks, a few feet above the surf, basking in the sun with outstretched legs.'

'On the hills, an ugly yellowish-brown species was equally common.'

Land Iguanas

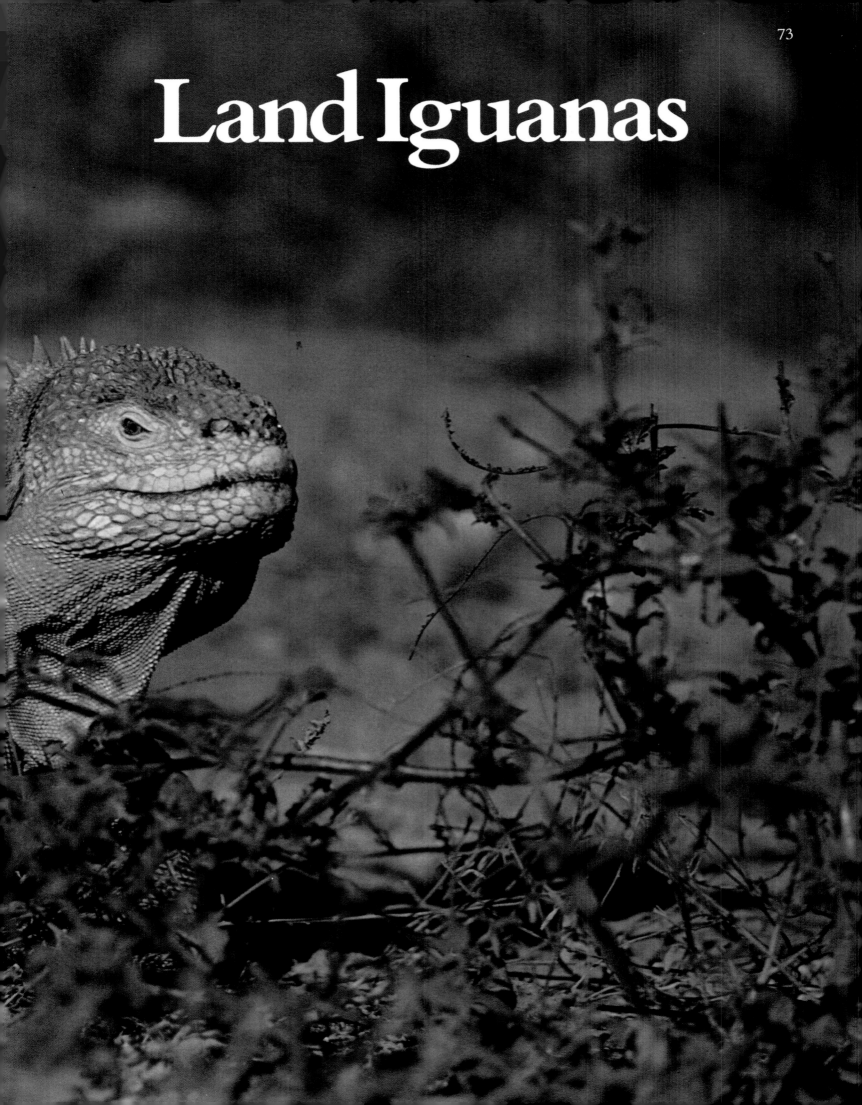

'In their movements they are lazy and half torpid. When not frightened, they slowly crawl along with tails and bellies dragging on the ground. They often stop, and doze for a minute or two, with closed eyes and hind legs spread out on the parched soil.'

'A remarkable genus of lizards'.

'They consume much of the succulent cactus.'

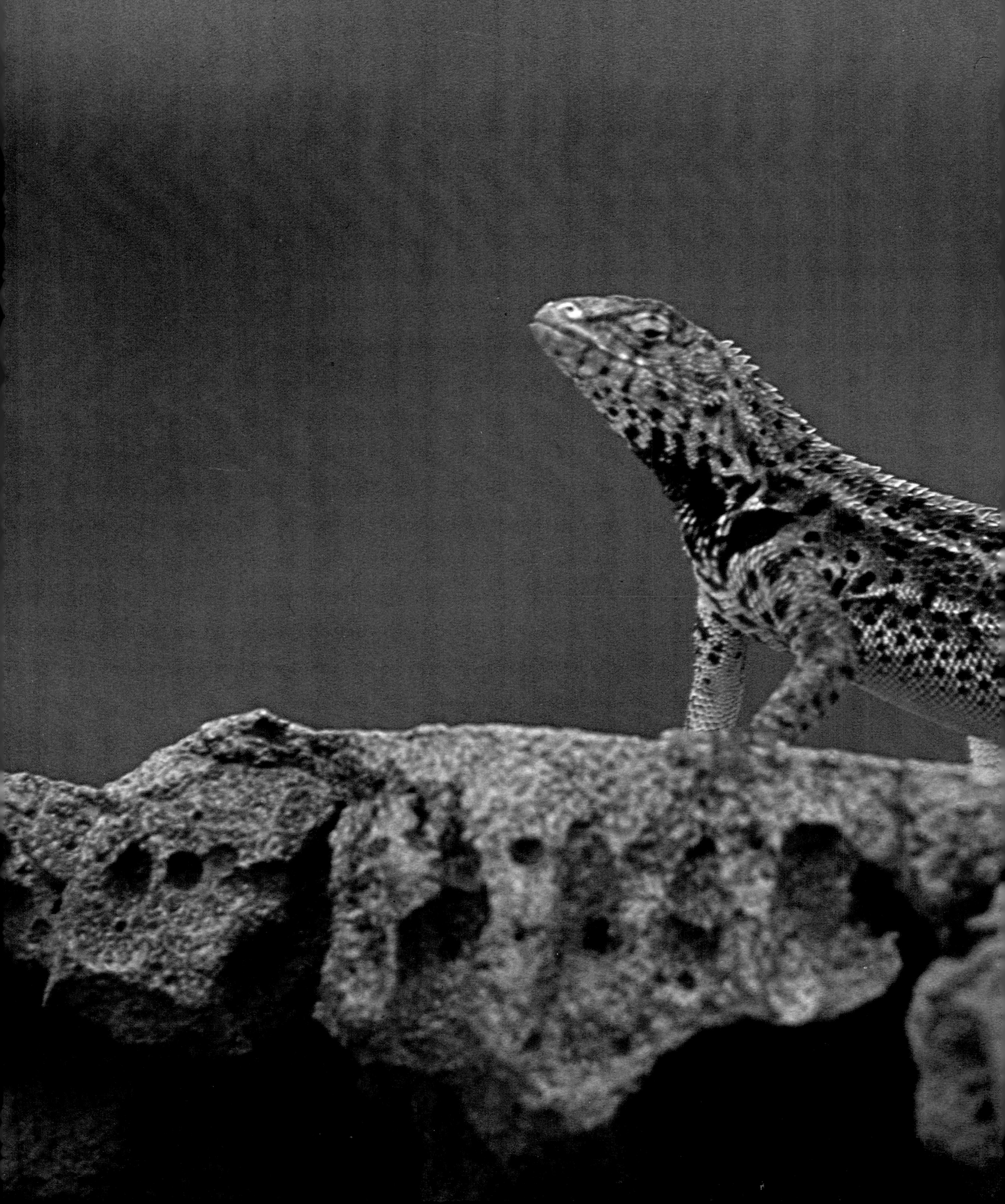

Lava Lizards

'They eat very deliberately, but do not chew their food.'

Finches

'Related to each other in the structure of their beaks, short tails, form of body, and plumage.'

Seals and Sea-lions

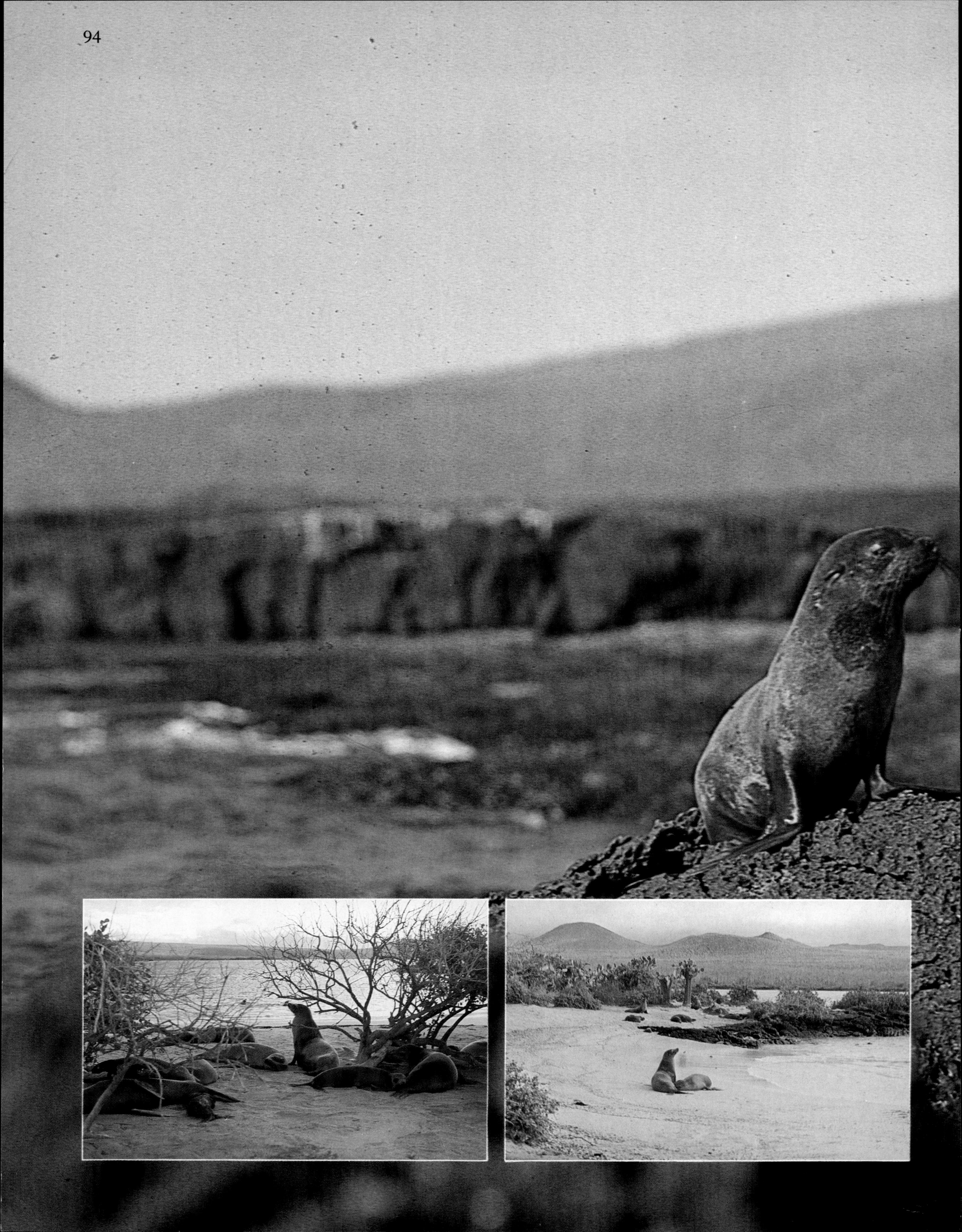

'During the greater part of our stay of a week, the sky was cloudless, and if the trade-wind failed for an hour, the heat became very oppressive. On two days, the thermometer within the tent stood for some hours at 93°; but in the open air, in the wind and sun, at only 85° The sand was extremely hot; the thermometer placed in some of a brown colour immediately rose to 137°, and how much above that it would have risen, I do not know, for it was not graduated any higher. The black sand felt much hotter, so that even in thick boots it was quite disagreeable to walk over it.'

'The natural history of these
islands is eminently curious.'

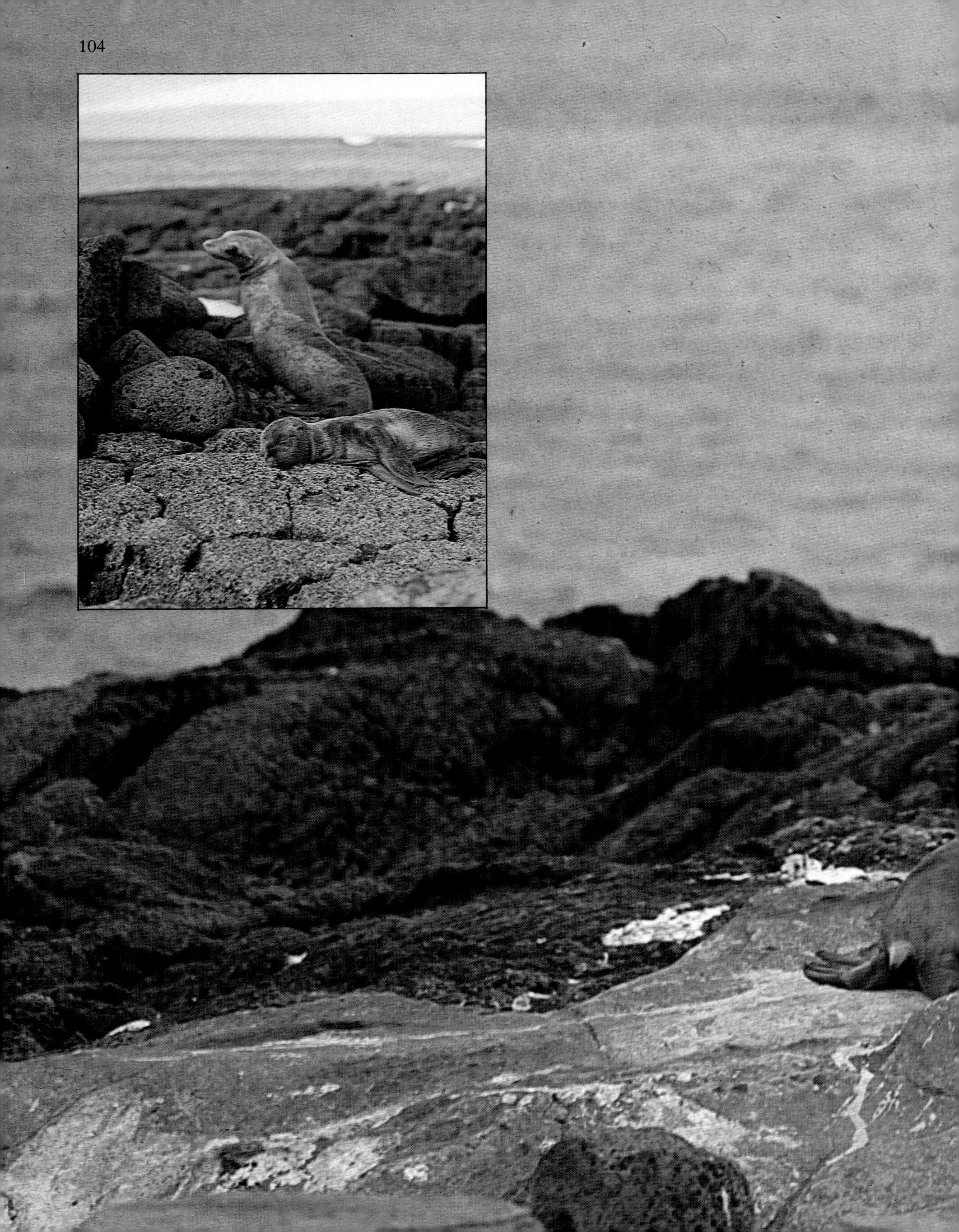

'Most of the organic productions
are aboriginal creations, found
nowhere else.'

'There is even a difference between the inhabitants of the different islands.'

Crabs

'The archipelago is a little
world within itself.'

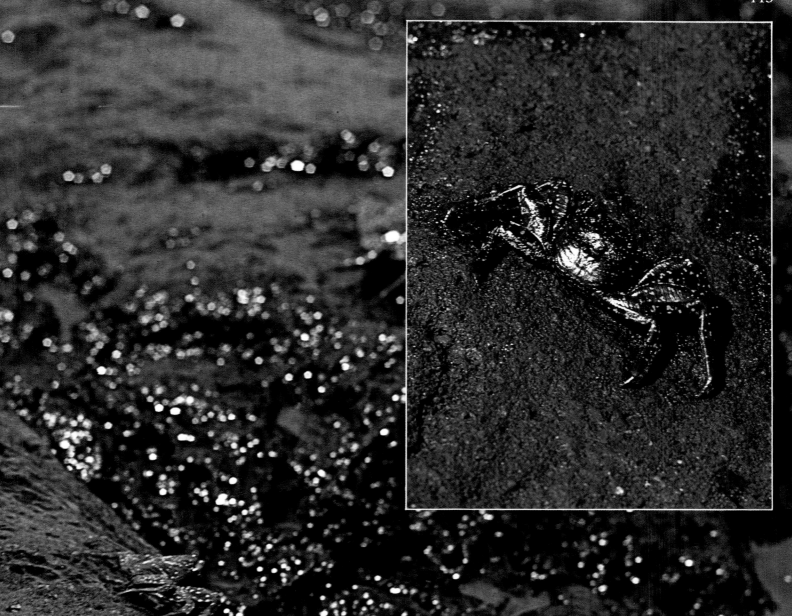

'Considering the small size of these islands we feel the more astonished at the number of their aboriginal beings, and at their confined range.'

Green Pacific Turtles

Birds

'Firstly, of a hawk, curiously
intermediate in structure between
a Buzzard and the American
group of carrion-feeding
Polybori.'

'Secondly, there are two owls,
representing the short-eared and
white barn-owls of Europe.'

'Thirdly, a wren, three tyrant fly-catchers.'

'And a dove.'

'I often tried, and very nearly
succeeded, in catching these birds
by their legs.'

'Formerly the birds appear to have been even tamer than at present.'

'It is surprising that they have not become wilder; for these islands during the last hundred and fifty years have been frequently visited by bucaniers and whalers.'

140

'The Totanus, and the gull, are
likewise duskier coloured than
their analogous species.'

'Of waders and water-birds I was
able to get only eleven kinds.'

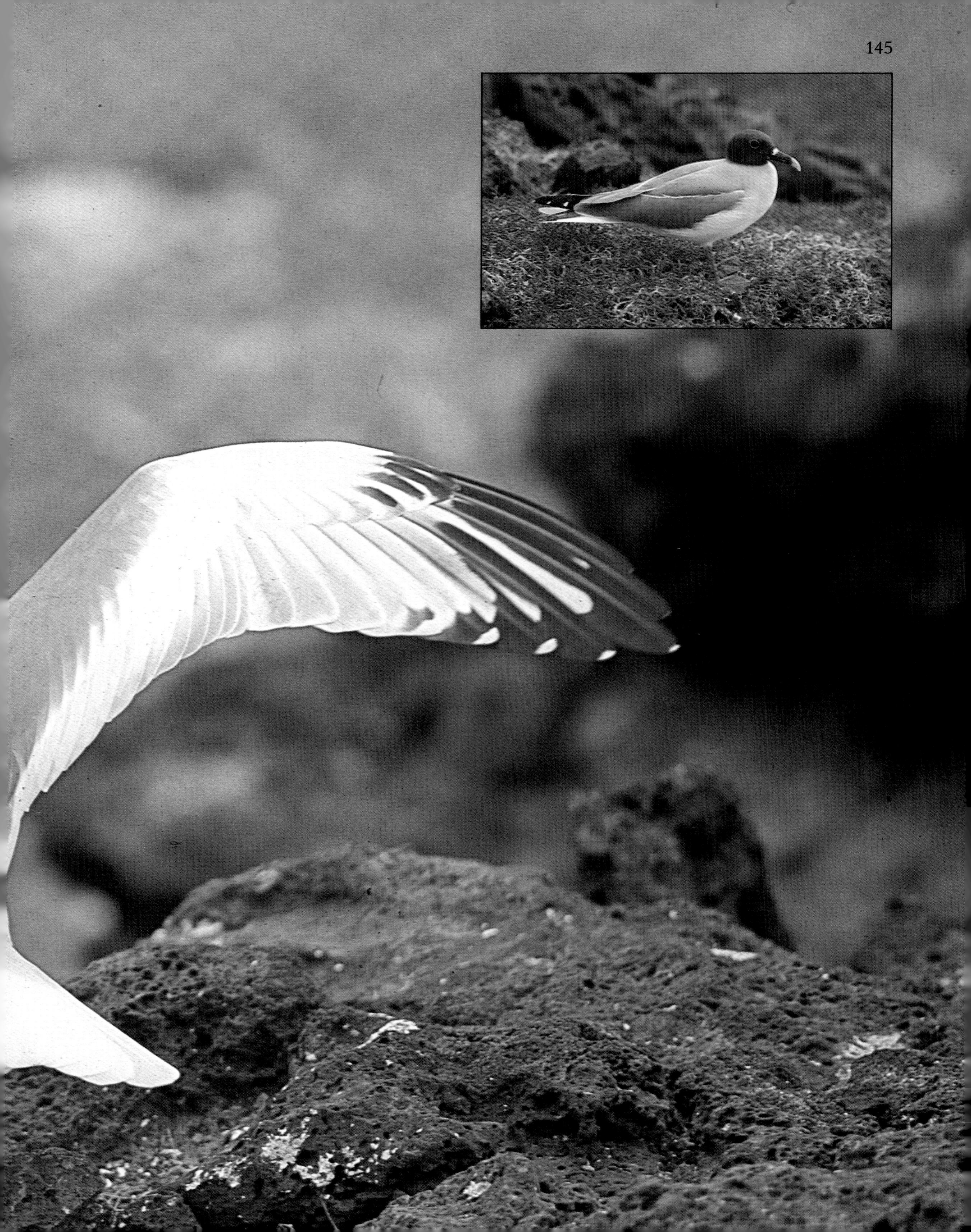

'Considering the wandering habits of the gulls,
I was surprised to find that the species
inhabiting these islands is peculiar.'

'The wildness of birds with regard to man, is a particular instinct directed against *him*.'

'It is not acquired by individual birds in a short time, even when much persecuted; but that in the course of successive generations it becomes hereditary.'

'What havoc the introduction of
any new beast of prey must cause
in a country, before the instincts
of the indigenous inhabitants have
become adapted to the stranger's
craft of power.'

'Only three (including a rail confined to the damp summits of the islands) are new species.'

'In regard to the wildness of birds towards man, there is no way of accounting for it, except as an inherited habit.'

'It allowed me to lift it from the ground whilst seated.'

'None of the birds are brilliantly coloured, as might have been expected in an equatorial district.'

'Hence it would appear probable, that the same causes which here make the immigrants of some species smaller, make most of the peculiar Galapageian species also smaller, as well as very generally more dusky coloured.'

'We may, therefore, conclude that
the usual gaudy colouring of the
intertropical productions, is not
related either to the heat or light
of those zones, but to some other
cause, perhaps to the conditions
of existence being generally
favourable to life.'

'The Galapagos Archipelago'

from Darwin's 'Voyage of the *Beagle*'

September 15th.—This archipelago consists of ten principal islands, of which five exceed the others in size. They are situated under the Equator, and between five and six hundred miles westward off the coast of America. They are all formed of volcanic rocks; a few fragments of granite curiously glazed and altered by the heat, can hardly be considered as an exception. Some of the craters, surmounting the larger islands, are of immense size, and they rise to a height of between three and four thousand feet. Their flanks are studded by innumerable smaller orifices. I scarcely hesitate to affirm, that there must be in the whole archipelago at least two thousand craters. These consist either of lava and scoriæ, or of finely-stratified, sandstone-like tuff. Most of the latter are beautifully symmetrical; they owe their origin to eruptions of volcanic mud without any lava: it is a remarkable circumstance that every one of the twenty-eight tuff-craters which were examined, had their southern sides either much lower than the other sides, or quite broken down and removed. As all these craters apparently have been formed when standing in the sea, and as the waves from the trade wind and the swell from the open Pacific here unite their forces on the southern coasts of all the islands, this singular uniformity in the broken state of the craters, composed of the soft and yielding tuff, is easily explained.

Considering that these islands are placed directly under the equator, the climate is far from being excessively hot; this seems chiefly caused by the singularly low temperature of the surrounding water, brought here by the great southern Polar current. Excepting during one short season, very little rain falls, and even then it is irregular; but the clouds generally hang low. Hence, whilst the lower parts of the islands are very sterile, the upper parts, at a height of a thousand feet and upwards, possess a damp climate and a tolerably luxuriant vegetation. This is especially the case on the windward sides of the islands, which first receive and condense the moisture from the atmosphere.

In the morning (17th) we landed on Chatham Island, which, like the others, rises with a tame and rounded outline, broken here and there by scattered hillocks, the remains of former craters. Nothing could be less inviting than the first appearance. A broken field of black basaltic lava, thrown into the most rugged waves, and crossed by great fissures, is every where covered by stunted, sun-burnt brushwood, which shows little signs of life. The dry and parched surface, being heated by the noon-day sun, gave to the air a close and sultry feeling, like that from a stove: we fancied even that the bushes smelt unpleasantly. Although I diligently tried to collect as many plants as possible, I succeeded in getting very few; and such wretched-looking little weeds would have better become an arctic than an equatorial Flora. The brushwood appears, from a short distance, as leafless as our trees during winter; and it was some time before I discovered that not only almost every plant was now in full leaf, but that the greater number were in flower. The commonest bush is one of the Euphorbiaceæ: an acacia a great odd-looking cactus are the only trees which afford any shade. After the season of heavy rains, the islands are said to appear for a short time partially green. The volcanic island of Fernando Noronha, placed in many respects under nearly similar conditions, is the only other country where I have seen a vegetation at all like this of the Galapagos islands.

The Beagle sailed round Chatham Island, and anchored in several bays. One night I slept on shore on a part of the island, where black truncated cones were extraordinarily numerous: from one small eminence I counted sixty of them, all surmounted by craters more or less perfect. The greater number consisted merely of a ring of red scoriæ or slags, cemented together: and their height above the plain of lava was not more than from fifty to a hundred feet: none had been very lately active. The entire surface of this part of the island seems to have been permeated, like a sieve, by the subterranean vapours: here and there the lava, whilst soft, has been blown into great bubbles; and in other parts, the tops of caverns similarly formed have fallen in, leaving circular pits with steep sides. From the regular form of the many craters, they gave to the country an artificial appearance, which vividly reminded me of those parts of Staffordshire, where the great iron-foundries are most numerous. The day was glowing hot, and the scrambling over the rough surface and through the intricate thickets, was very fatiguing; but I was well repaid by the strange Cyclopean scene. As I was walking along I met two large tortoises, each of which must have weighed at least two hundred pounds: one was eating a piece of cactus, and as I approached, it stared at me and slowly stalked away; the other gave a deep hiss, and drew in its head. These huge reptiles, surrounded by the black lava, the leafless shrubs, and large cacti, seemed to my fancy like some antediluvian animals. The few dull-coloured birds cared no more for me, than they did for the great tortoises.

September 23rd—The Beagle proceeded to Charles Island. This archipelago has long been frequented, first by the Bucaniers, and latterly by whalers, but it is only within the last six years, that a small colony has been established here. The inhabitants are between two and three hundred in number: they are nearly all people of colour, who have been banished for political crimes from the Republic of the Equator, of which Quito is the capital. The settlement is placed about four and a half miles inland, and at a height probably of a thousand feet. In the first part of the road we passed through leafless thickets, as in Chatham Island. Higher up, the woods gradually became greener; and as soon as we crossed the ridge of the island, we were cooled by a fine southerly breeze, and our sight refreshed by a green and thriving vegetation. In this upper region coarse grasses and ferns abound; but there are no tree-ferns: I saw nowhere any member of the Palm family, which is the more singular, as 360 miles northward, Cocos Island takes its name from the number of cocoa-nuts. The houses are irregularly scattered over a flat space of ground, which is cultivated with sweet potatoes and bananas. It will not easily be imagined how pleasant the sight of black mud was to us, after having been so long accustomed to the parched soil of Peru and northern Chile. The inhabitants, although complaining of poverty, obtain, without much trouble, the means of subsistence. In the woods there are many wild pigs and goats; but the staple article of animal food is supplied by the tortoises. Their numbers have of course been greatly reduced in this island, but the people yet count on two days' hunting giving them food for the rest of the week. It is said that formerly single vessels have taken away as many as seven hundred, and that the ship's company of a frigate some years since brought down in one day two hundred tortoises to the beach.

September 29th.—We doubled the south-west extremity of Albemarle Island, and the next day were nearly becalmed between it and Narborough Island. Both are covered with immense deluges of black naked lava, which have flowed either over the rims of the great caldrons, like pitch over the rim of a pot in which it has been boiled, or have burst forth from smaller orifices on the flanks; in their descent they have spread over miles of the sea-coast. On both of these islands, eruptions are known to have taken place; and in Albemarle, we saw a small jet of smoke curling from the summit of one of the great craters. In the evening we anchored in Bank's Cove, in Albemarle Island. The next morning I went out walking. To the south of the broken tuff-crater, in which the Beagle was anchored, there was another beautifully symmetrical one of an elliptic form; its longer axis was a little less than a mile, and its depth about 500 feet. At its bottom there was a shallow lake, in the middle of which a tiny crater formed an islet. The day was overpoweringly hot, and the lake looked clear and blue: I hurried down the cindery slope, and choked with dust eagerly tasted the water—but, to my sorrow, I found it salt as brine.

The rocks on the coast abounded with great black lizards, between three and four feet long; and on the hills, an ugly yellowish-brown species was equally common. We saw many of this latter kind, some clumsily running out of our way, and others shuffling into their burrows. I shall presently describe in detail the habits of both these reptiles. The whole of this northern part of Albemarle Island is miserably sterile.

October 8th.—We arrived at James Island: this island, as well as Charles Island, were long since thus named after our kings of the Stuart line. Mr. Bynoe, myself, and our servants were left here for a week, with provisions and a tent, whilst the Beagle went for water. We found here a party of Spaniards, who had been sent from Charles Island to dry fish, and to salt tortoise-meat. About six miles inland, and at the height of nearly 2000 feet, a hovel had been built in which two men lived, who were employed in catching tortoises, whilst the others were fishing on the coast. I paid this party two visits, and slept there one night. As in the other islands, the lower region was covered by nearly leafless bushes, but the trees were here of a larger growth than elsewhere, several being two feet and some even two feet nine inches in diameter. The upper region being kept damp by the clouds, supports a green and flourishing vegetation. So damp was the ground, that there were large beds of a coarse cyperus, in which great numbers of a very small water-rail lived and bred.

While staying in this upper region, we lived entirely upon tortoise-meat: the breast-plate roasted (as the Gauchos do *carne con cuero*), with the flesh on it, is very good; and the young tortoises make excellent soup; but otherwise the meat to my taste is indifferent.

One day we accompanied a party of the Spaniards in their whale-boat to a salina, or lake from which salt is procured. After landing, we had a very rough walk over a rugged field of recent lava, which has almost surrounded a tuff-crater, at the bottom of which the salt-lake lies. The water is only three or four inches deep, and rests on a layer of beautifully crystallized, white salt. The lake is quite circular, and is fringed with a border of bright green succulent plants; the almost precipitous walls of the crater are clothed with wood, so that the scene was altogether both picturesque and curious. A few years since, the sailors belonging to a sealing-vessel murdered their captain in this quiet spot; and we saw his skull lying among the bushes.

During the greater part of our stay of a week, the sky was cloudless, and if the trade-wind failed for an hour, the heat became very oppressive. On two days, the thermometer within the tent stood for some hours at 93°; but in the open air, in the wind and sun, at only 85°. The sand was extremely hot; the thermometer placed in some of a brown colour immediately rose to 137°, and how much above that it would have risen, I do not know, for it was not graduated any higher. The black sand felt much hotter, so that even in thick boots it was quite disagreeable to walk over it.

The natural history of these islands is eminently curious, and well deserves attention. Most of the organic productions are aboriginal creations, found nowhere else; there is even a difference between the inhabitants of the different islands; yet all show a marked relationship with those of America, though separated from that continent by an open space of ocean, between 500 and 600 miles in width. The archipelago is a little world within itself, or rather a satellite attached to America, whence it has derived a few stray colonists, and has received the general character of its indigenous productions. Considering the small size of these islands, we feel the more astonished at the number of their aboriginal beings, and at their confined range. Seeing every height crowned with its crater, and the boundaries of most of the lava-streams still distinct, we are led to believe that within a period, geologically recent, the unbroken ocean was here spread out. Hence, both in space and time, we seem to be brought somewhat near to that great fact—that mystery of mysteries—the first appearance of new beings on this earth.

Of terrestrial mammals, there is only one which must be considered as indigenous, namely, a mouse (Mus Galapagoensis), and this is confined, as far as I could ascertain, to Chatham island, the most easterly island of the group. It belongs, as I am informed by Mr. Waterhouse, to a division of the family of mice characteristic of America. At James island, there is a rat sufficiently distinct from the common kind to have been named and described by Mr. Waterhouse; but as it belongs to the old-world division of the family, and as this island has been frequented by ships for the last hundred and fifty years, I can hardly doubt that this rat is merely a variety, produced by the new and peculiar climate, food, and soil, to which it has been subjected. Although no one has a right to speculate without distinct facts, yet even with respect to the Chatham island mouse, it should be borne in mind, that it may possibly be an American species imported here; for I have seen, in a most unfrequented part of the Pampas, a native mouse living in the roof of a newly-built hovel, and therefore its transportation in a vessel is not improbable:

analogous facts have been observed by Dr. Richardson in in North America.

Of land-birds I obtained twenty-six kinds, all peculiar to the group and found nowhere else, with the exception of one lark-like finch from North America (Dolichonyx oryzivorus), which ranges on that continent as far north as 54°, and generally frequents marshes. The other twenty-five birds consist, firstly, of a hawk, curiously intermediate in structure between a Buzzard and the American group of carrion-feeding Polybori: and with these latter birds it agrees most closely in every habit and even tone of voice. Secondly, there are two owls, representing the short-eared and white barn-owls of Europe. Thirdly, a wren, three tyrant fly-catchers (two of them species of Pyrocephalus, one or both of which would be ranked by some ornithologists as only varieties), and a dove—all analogous to, but distinct from, American species. Fourthly, a swallow, which though differing from the Progne purpurea of both Americas, only in being rather duller coloured, smaller, and slenderer, is considered by Mr. Gould as specifically distinct. Fifthly, there are three species of mocking-thrush—a form highly characteristic of America. The remaining land-birds form a most singular group of finches, related to each other in the structure of their beaks, short tails, form of body, and plumage: there are thirteen species, which Mr. Gould has divided into four sub-groups. All these species are peculiar to this archipelago; and so is the whole group, with the exception of one species of the sub-group, Cactornis, lately brought from Bow island, in the Low Archipelago. Of Cactornis, the two species may be often seen climbing about the flowers of the great cactus-trees; but all the other species of this group of finches, mingled together in flocks, feed on the dry and sterile ground of the lower districts. The males of all, or certainly of the greater number, are jet black; and the females (with perhaps one or two exceptions) are brown. The most curious fact is the perfect gradation in the size of the beaks in the different species of Geospiza, from one as large as that of a hawfinch to that of a chaffinch, and (if Mr. Gould is right in including his sub-group, Certhidea, in the main group), even that of a warbler. Seeing this gradation and diversity of structure in one small, intimately related group of birds, one might really fancy that from an original paucity of birds in this archipelago, one species had been taken and modified for different ends. In a like manner it might be fancied that a bird originally a buzzard, had been induced here to undertake the office of the carrion-feeding Polybori of the American continent.

Of waders and water-birds I was able to get only eleven kinds, and of these only three (including a rail confined to the damp summits of the islands) are new species. Considering the wandering habits of the gulls, I was surprised to find that the species inhabiting these islands is peculiar, but allied to one from the southern parts of South America. The far greater peculiarity of the land-birds, namely, twenty-five out of twenty-six being new species or at least new races, compared with the waders and web-footed birds, is in accordance with the greater range which these latter orders have in all parts of the world. We shall hereafter see this law of aquatic forms, whether marine or fresh-water, being less peculiar at any given point of the earth's surface than the terrestrial forms of the same classes, strikingly illustrated in the shells, and in a lesser degree in the insects of this archipelago.

Two of the waders are rather smaller than the same species brought from other places: the swallow is also smaller, though it is doubtful whether or not it is distinct from its analogue. The two owls, the two tyrant fly-catchers (Pyrocephalus) and

the dove, are also smaller than the analogous but distinct species, to which they are most nearly related; on the other hand, the gull is rather larger. The two owls, the swallow, all three species of mocking-thrush, the dove in its separate colours though not in its whole plumage, the Totanus, and the gull, are likewise duskier coloured than their analogous species; and in the case of the mocking-thrush and Totanus, than any other species of the two genera. With the exception of a wren a fine yellow breast, and of a tyrant fly-catcher with a scarlet tuft and breast, none of the birds are brilliantly coloured, as might have been expected in an equatorial district. Hence it would appear probable, that the same causes which here make the immigrants of some species smaller, make most of the peculiar Galapageian species also smaller, as well as very generally more dusky coloured. All the plants have a wretched, weedy appearance, and I did not see one beautiful flower. The insects, again, are small sized and dull coloured, and as Mr. Waterhouse informs me, there is nothing in their general appearance which would have led him to imagine that they had come from under the equator. The birds, plants, and insects have a desert character, and are not more brilliantly coloured than those from southern Patagonia; we may, therefore, conclude that the usual gaudy colouring of the intertropical productions, is not related either to the heat or light of those zones, but to some other cause, perhaps to the conditions of existence being generally favourable to life.

We will now turn to the order of reptiles, which gives the most striking character to the zoology of these islands. The species are not numerous, but the numbers of individuals of each species are extraordinarily great. There is one small lizard belonging to a South American genus, and two species (and probably more) of the Amblyrhynchus—a genus confined to the Galapagos islands. There is one snake which is numerous; it is identical, as I am informed by M. Bibron, with the Psammophis Temminckii from Chile. Of sea-turtle I believe there is more than one species; and of tortoises there are, as we shall presently show, two or three species or races. Of toads and frogs there are none: I was surprised at this, considering how well suited for them the temperate and damp upper woods appeared to be. It recalled to my mind the remark made by Bory St. Vincent, namely, that none of this family are found on any of the volcanic islands in the great oceans. As far as I can ascertain from various works, this seems to hold good throughout the Pacific, and even in the large islands of the Sandwich archipelago. Mauritius offers an apparent exception, where I saw the Rana Mascariensis in abundance: this frog is said now to inhabit the Seychelles, Madagascar, and Bourbon; but on the other hand, Du Bois, in his voyage in 1669, states that there were no reptiles in Bourbon except tortoises; and the Officier du Roi asserts that before 1768 it had been attempted, without success, to introduce frogs into Mauritius—I presume, for the purpose of eating: hence it may be well doubted whether this frog is an aboriginal of these islands. The absence of the frog family in the oceanic islands is the more remarkable, when contrasted with the case of lizards, which swarm on most of the smallest islands. May this difference not be caused, by the greater facility with which the eggs of lizards, protected by calcareous shells, might be transported through salt-water, than could the slimy spawn of frogs?

I will first describe the habits of the tortoise (Testudo nigra, formerly called Indica), which has been so frequently alluded to. These animals are found, I believe, on all the islands of the Archipelago; certainly on the greater number. They frequent in preference the high damp parts, but they likewise live in the lower and arid districts. I have already shown, from the numbers which have been caught in a single day, how very numerous they must be. Some grow to an immense size: Mr. Lawson, an Englishman, and vice-governor of the colony, told us that he had seen several so large, that it required six or eight men to lift them from the ground; and that some had afforded as much as two hundred pounds of meat. The old males are the largest, the females rarely growing to so great a size: the male can readily be distinguished from the female by the greater length of its tail. The tortoises which live on those islands where there is no water, or in the lower and arid parts of the others, feed chiefly on the succulent cactus. Those which frequent the higher and damp regions, eat the leaves of various trees, a kind of berry (called guayavita) which is acid and austere, and likewise a pale green filamentous lichen (Usnera plicata), that hangs in tresses from the boughs of the trees.

The tortoise is very fond of water, drinking large quantities, and wallowing in the mud. The larger islands alone possess springs, and these are always situated towards the central parts, and at a considerable height. The tortoises, therefore, which frequent the lower districts, when thirsty, are obliged to travel from a long distance. Hence broad and well-beaten paths branch off in every direction from the wells down to the sea-coast; and the Spaniards by following them up, first discovered the watering-places. When I landed at Chatham Island, I could not imagine what animal travelled so methodically along well-chosen tracks. Near the springs it was a curious spectacle to behold many of these huge creatures, one set eagerly travelling onwards with out-stretched necks, and another set returning, after having drunk their fill. When the tortoise arrives at the spring, quite regardless of any spectator, he buries his head in the water above his eyes, and greedily swallows great mouthfuls, at the rate of about ten in a minute. The inhabitants say each animal stays three or four days in the neighbourhood of the water, and then returns to the lower country; but they differed respecting the frequency of these visits. The animal probably regulates them according to the nature of the food on which it has lived. It is, however, certain, that tortoises can subsist even on those islands, where there is no other water than what falls during a few rainy days in the year.

I believe it is well ascertained, that the bladder of the frog acts as a reservoir for the moisture necessary to its existence: such seems to be the case with the tortoise. For some time after a visit to the springs, their urinary bladders are distended with fluid, which is said gradually to decrease in volume, and to become less pure. The inhabitants, when walking in the lower district, and overcome with thirst, often take advantage of this circumstance, and drink the contents of the bladder if full: in one I saw killed, the fluid was quite limpid, and had only a very slightly bitter taste. The inhabitants, however, always first drink the water in the pericardium, which is described as being best.

The tortoises, when purposely moving towards any point, travel by night and day, and arrive at their journey's end much sooner than would be expected. The inhabitants, from observing marked individuals, consider that they travel a distance of about eight miles in two or three days. One large tortoise, which I watched, walked at the rate of sixty yards in ten minutes, that is 360 yards in the hour, or four miles a day,—allowing a little time for it to eat on the road. During the breeding season, when the male and female are together, the male utters a hoarse roar or bellowing, which, it is said, can be heard at the distance of more than a hundred yards. The female never uses her voice, and the male only at these times; so that when the people hear this noise, they know that the two are together. They were at this time (October) laying their eggs. The female, where the soil is sandy, deposits them together, and covers them up with sand; but where the ground is rocky she drops them indiscriminately in any hole: Mr. Bynoe found seven placed in a fissure. The egg is white and spherical; one which I measured was seven inches and three-eighths in circumference, and therefore larger than a hen's egg. The young tortoises, as soon as they are hatched, fall a prey in great numbers to the carrion-feeding buzzard. The old ones seem generally to die from accidents, as from falling down precipices: at least, several of the inhabitants told me, that they had never found one dead without some evident cause.

The inhabitants believe that these animals are absolutely deaf; certainly they do not overhear a person walking close behind them. I was always amused when overtaking one of these great monsters, as it was quietly pacing along, to see how suddenly, the instant I passed, it would draw in its head and legs, and uttering a deep hiss fall to the ground with a heavy sound, as if struck dead. I frequently got on their backs, and then giving a few raps on the hinder part of their shells, they would rise up and walk away;—but I found it very difficult to keep my balance. The flesh of this animal is largely employed, both fresh and salted; and a beautifully clear oil is prepared from the fat. When a tortoise is caught, the man makes a slit in the skin near its tail, so as to see inside its body, whether the fat under the dorsal plate is thick. If it is not, the animal is liberated; and it is said to recover soon from this strange operation. In order to secure the tortoises, it is not sufficient to turn them like turtles, for they are often able to get on their legs again.

There can be little doubt that this tortoise is an aboriginal inhabitant of the Galapagos; for it is found on all, or nearly all, the islands, even on some of the smaller ones where there is no water; had it been an imported species, this would hardly have been the case in a group which has been so little frequented. Moreover, the old Bucaniers found this tortoise in greater numbers even than at present: Wood and Rogers also, in 1708, say that it is the opinion of the Spaniards, that it is found nowhere else in this quarter of the world. It is now widely distributed; but it may be questioned whether it is in any other place an aboriginal. The bones of a tortoise at Mauritius, associated with those of the extinct Dodo, have generally been considered as belonging to this tortoise: if this had been so, undoubtedly it must have been there indigenous; but M. Bibron informs me that he believes that it was distinct, as the species now living there certainly is.

The Amblyrhynchus, a remarkable genus of lizards, is confined to this archipelago: there are two species, resembling each other in general form, one being terrestrial and the other aquatic. This latter species (A. cristatus) was first characterised by Mr. Bell, who well foresaw, from its short, broad head, and strong claws of equal length, that its habits of life would turn out very peculiar, and different from those of its nearest ally, the Iguana. It is extremely common on all the islands throughout the group, and lives exclusively on the rocky sea-beaches, being never found, at least I never saw one, even ten yards in-shore. It is a hideous-looking creature, of a dirty black colour, stupid, and sluggish in its movements. The usual length of a full-grown one is about a yard, but there are some even four feet long; a large one weighed twenty pounds: on the island of Albemarle they seem to grow to a greater size than elsewhere. Their tails are flattened sideways, and all four feet partially webbed. They are occasionally seen some hundred yards from the shore, swimming about; and Captain Collnett, in his Voyage, says, "They go to sea in herds a-fishing, and sun themselves on the rocks; and may be called alligators in miniature." It must not, however, be supposed that they live on fish. When in the water this lizard swims with perfect ease and quickness, by a serpentine movement of its body and flattened tail—the legs being motionless and closely collapsed on its sides. A seaman on board sank one, with a heavy weight attached to it, thinking thus to kill it directly; but when, an hour afterwards, he drew up the line, it was quite active. Their limbs and strong claws are admirably adapted for crawling over the rugged and fissured masses of lava, which everywhere form the coast. In such situations, a group of six or seven of these hideous reptiles may oftentimes be seen on the black rocks, a few feet above the surf, basking in the sun with outstretched legs.

I opened the stomachs of several, and found them largely distended with minced sea-weed (Ulvæ), which grows in thin foliaceous expansions of a bright green or a dull red colour. I do not recollect having observed this sea-weed in any quantity on the tidal rocks; and I have reason to believe it grows at the bottom of the sea, at some little distance from the coast. If such be the case, the object of these animals occasionally going out to sea is explained. The stomach contained nothing but the sea-weed. Mr. Bynoe, however, found a piece of a crab in one; but this might have got in accidently, in the same manner as I have seen a caterpillar, in the midst of some lichen, in the paunch of a tortoise. The intestines were large, as in other herbivorous animals. The nature of this lizard's food, as well as the structure of its tail and feet, and the fact of its having been seen voluntarily swimming out at sea, absolutely prove its aquatic habits; yet there is in this respect one strange anomaly, namely, that when frightened it will not enter the water. Hence it is easy to drive these lizards down to any little point overhanging the sea, where they will sooner allow a person to catch hold of their tails than jump into the water. They do not seem to have any notion of biting; but when much frightened they squirt a drop of fluid from each nostril. I threw one several times as far as I could, into a deep pool left by the retiring tide; but it invariably returned in a direct line to the spot where I stood. It swam near the bottom, with a very graceful and rapid movement, and occasionally aided itself over the uneven ground with its feet. As soon as it arrived near the edge, but still being under water, it tried to conceal itself in the tufts of sea-weed, or it entered some crevice. As soon as it thought the danger was past, it crawled out on the dry rocks, and shuffled away as quickly as it could. I several times caught this same lizard, by driving it down to a point, and though possessed of such perfect powers of diving and swimming, nothing would induce it to enter the water; and as often as I threw it in, it returned in the manner above described. Perhaps this singular piece of apparent stupidity may be accounted for by the circumstance, that this reptile has no enemy whatever on shore, whereas at sea it must often fall a prey to the numerous sharks. Hence, probably, urged by a fixed and hereditary instinct that the shore is its place of safety, whatever the emergency may be, it there takes refuge.

During our visit (in October), I saw extremely few small individuals of this species, and none I should think under a year old. From this circumstance it seems probable that the breeding season had not then commenced. I asked several of the inhabitants if they knew where it laid its eggs: they said that they knew nothing of its propagation although well acquainted with the eggs of the land kind—a fact, considering how very common this lizard is, not a little extraordinary.

We will now turn to the terrestrial species (A. Demarlii). with a round tail, and toes without webs. This lizard, instead of being found like the other on all the islands, is confined to the central part of the archipelago, namely to Albemarle, James, Barrington, and Indefatigable islands. To the southward, in Charles, Hood, and Chatham islands, and to the northward, in Towers, Bindloes, and Abingdon, I neither saw nor heard of any. It would appear as if it had been created in the centre of the archipelago, and thence had been dispersed only to a certain distance. Some of these lizards inhabit the high and damp parts of the islands, but they are much more numerous in the lower and sterile districts near the coast. I cannot give a more forcible proof of their numbers, than by stating that when we were left at James Island, we could not for some time find a spot free from their burrows on which to pitch our single tent. Like their brothers the sea-kind, they are ugly animals, of a yellowish orange beneath, and of a brownish red colour above: from their low facial angle they have a singularly stupid appearance. They are, perhaps, of a rather less size than the marine species; but several of them weighed between ten and fifteen pounds. In their movements they are lazy and half torpid. When not frightened, they slowly crawl along with their tails and bellies dragging on the ground. They often stop, and doze for a minute or two, with closed eyes and hind legs spread out on the parched soil.

They inhabit burrows, which they sometimes make between fragments of lava, but more generally on level patches of the soft sandstone-like tuff. The holes do not appear to be very deep, and they enter the ground at a small angle; so that when walking over these lizard-warrens, the soil is constantly giving way, much to the annoyance of the tired walker. This animal, when making its burrow, works alternately the opposite sides of its body. One front leg for a short time scratches up the soil, and throws it towards the hind foot, which is well placed so as to heave it beyond the mouth of the hole. That side of the body being tired, the other takes up the task, and so on alternately. I watched one for a long time, till half its body was buried; I then walked up and pulled it by the tail; at this it was greatly astonished, and soon shuffled up to see what was the matter; and then stared me in the face, as much as to say, 'What made you pull my tail?'

They feed by day, and do not wander far from their burrows; if frightened, they rush to them with a most awkward gait. Except when running down hill, they cannot move very fast, apparently from the lateral position of their legs. They are not at all timorous: when attentively watching any one, they curl their tails, raising themselves on their front legs, nod their heads vertically, with a quick movement, and try to look very fierce: but in reality they are not at all so; if one just stamps on the ground, down go their tails, and off they shuffle as quickly as they can. I have frequently observed small fly-eating lizards, when watching anything, nod their heads in precisely the same manner; but I do not at all know for what purpose. If this Amblyrhynchus is held and plagued with a stick, it will bite it very severely; but I caught many by the tail, and they never tried to bite me. If two are placed on the ground and held together, they will fight, and bite each other till blood is drawn.

The individuals, and they are the greater number, which inhabit the lower country, can scarcely taste a drop of water throughout the year; but they consume much of the succulent cactus, the branches of which are occasionally broken off by the wind. I several times threw a piece to two or three of them when together; and it was amusing enough to see them trying to seize and carry it away in their mouths, like so many hungry dogs with a bone. They eat very deliberately, but do not chew their food. The little birds are aware how harmless these creatures are: I have seen one of the thick-billed finches picking at one end of a piece of cactus (which is much relished by all the animals of the lower region), whilst a lizard was eating at the other end; and afterwards the little bird with the utmost indifference hopped on the back of the reptile.

I opened the stomachs of several, and found them full of vegetable fibres and leaves of different trees, especially of an acacia. In the upper region they live chiefly on the acid and astringent berries of the guayavita, under which trees I have seen these lizards and the huge tortoises feeding together. To obtain the acacia-leaves they crawl up the low stunted trees; and it is not uncommon to see a pair quietly browsing, whilst seated on a branch several feet above the ground. These lizards, when cooked, yield a white meat, which is liked by those whose stomachs soar above all prejudices. Humboldt has remarked that in intertropical South America, all lizards which inhabit dry regions are esteemed delicacies for the table. The inhabitants state that those which inhabit the upper damp parts drink water, but that the others do not, like the tortoises, travel up for it from the lower sterile country. At the time of our visit, the females had within their bodies numerous, large, elongated eggs, which they lay in their burrows: the inhabitants seek them for food.

These two species of Amblyrhynchus agree, as I have already stated, in their general structure, and in many of their habits. Neither have that rapid movement, so characteristic of the genera Lacerta and Iguana. They are both herbivorous, although the kind of vegetation on which they feed is so very different. Mr. Bell has given the name to the genus from the shortness of the snout; indeed, the form of the mouth may almost be compared to that of the tortoise: one is led to suppose that this is an adaptation to their herbivorous appetites. It is very interesting thus to find a well-charaterized genus, having its marine and terrestrial species, belonging to so confined a portion of the world. The aquatic species is by far the most remarkable, because it is the only existing lizard which lives on marine vegetable productions. As I at first observed, these islands are not so remarkable for the number of the species of reptiles, as for that of the individuals; when we remember the well-beaten paths made by the thousands of huge tortoises—the many turtles—the great warrens of the terrestrial Amblyrhynchus—and the groups of the marine species basking on the coast-rocks of every island—we must admit that there is no other quarter of the world where this Order replaces the herbivorous mammalia in so extraordinary a manner. The geologist on hearing this will probably refer back in his mind to the Secondary epochs, when lizards, some herbivorous, some carnivorous, and of dimensions comparable only with our existing whales, swarmed on the land and in the sea. It is, therefore, worthy of his observation, that this archipelago, instead of possessing a humid climate and rank vegetation, cannot be considered otherwise than extremely arid, and, for an equatorial region, remarkably temperate.

To finish with the zoology: the fifteen kinds of sea-fish which I procured here are all new species; they belong to twelve genera, all widely distributed, with the exception of Prionotus, of which the four previously known species live on the eastern side of America. Of land-shells I collected sixteen kinds (and two marked varieties), of which, with the exception of one Helix found at Tahiti, all are peculiar to this archipelago: a single fresh-water shell (Paludina) is common to Tahiti and Van Diemen's Land. Mr. Cuming, before our voyage, procured here ninety species of sea-shells, and this does not include several species not yet specifically examined, of Trochus, Turbo, Monodonta, and Nassa. He has been kind enough to give me the following interesting results: of the ninety shells, no less than forty-seven are unknown elsewhere—a wonderful fact, con-

sidering how widely distributed sea-shells generally are. Of the forty-three shells found in other parts of the world, twenty-five inhabit the western coast of America, and of these eight are distinguishable as varieties; the remaining eighteen (including one variety) were found by Mr. Cuming in the Low archipelago, and some of them also at the Philippines. This fact of shells from islands in the central parts of the Pacific occurring here, deserves notice, for not one single sea-shell is known to be common to the islands of that ocean and to the west coast of America. The space of open sea running north and south off the west coast, separates two quite distinct conchological provinces; but at the Galapagos Archipelago we have a halting-place, where many new forms have been created, and whither these two great conchological provinces have each sent several colonists. The American province has also sent here representative species; for there is a Galapageian species of Monoceros, a genus only found on the west coast of America; and there are Galapageian species of Fissurella and Cancellaria, genera common on the west coast, but not found (as I am informed by Mr. Cuming) in the central islands of the Pacific. On the other hand, there are Galapageian species of Oniscia and Stylifer, genera common to the West Indies and to the Chinese and Indian seas, but not found either on the west coast of America or in the central Pacific. I may here add, that after the comparison by Messrs. Cuming and Hinds of about 2000 shells from the eastern and western coasts of America, only one single shell was found in common, namely, the Purpura patula, which inhabits the West Indies, the coast of Panama, and the Galapagos. We have, therefore, in this quarter of the world, three great conchological sea-provinces, quite distinct, though surprisingly near each other, being separated by long north and south spaces either of land or of open sea.

I took great pains in collecting the insects, but, excepting Tierra del Fuego, I never saw in this respect so poor a country. Even in the upper and damp region I procured very few, excepting some minute Diptera and Hymenoptera, mostly of common mundane forms. As before remarked, the insects, for a tropical region, are of very small size and dull colours. Of beetles I collected twenty-five species (excluding a Dermestes and Corynetes imported, wherever a ship touches); of these, two belong to the Harpalidæ, two to the Hydrophilidæ, nine to three families of the Heteromera, and the remaining twelve to as many different families. This circumstance of insects (and I may add plants), where few in number, belonging to many different families, is I believe, very general. Mr. Waterhouse, who has published an account of the insects of this archipelago, and to whom I am indebted for the above details, informs me that there are several new genera; and that of the genera not new, one or two are American, and the rest of mundane distribution. With the exception of a wood-feeding Apate, and of one or probably two water-beetles from the American continent, all the species appear to be new.

The botany of this group is fully as interesting as the zoology. Dr. J. Hooker will soon publish in the 'Linnean Transactions' a full account of the Flora, and I am much indebted to him for the following details. Of flowering plants there are, as far as at present is known, 185 species, and 40 cryptogamic species, making together 225; of this number I was fortunate enough to bring home 193. Of the flowering plants, 100 are new species, and are probably confined to this archipelago. Dr. Hooker conceives that, of the plants not so confined, at least 10 species found near the cultivated ground at Charles Island, have been imported. It is, I think, surprising that more American species have not been introduced naturally, considering that the distance is only between 500 and 600 miles from the continent; and that (according to Collnett, p. 58) drift-wood, bamboos, canes, and the nuts of a palm, are often washed on the south-eastern shores. The proportion of 100 flowering plants out of 185 (or 175 excluding the imported weeds) being new, is sufficient, I conceive, to make the Galapagos Archipelago a distinct botanical province; but this Flora is not nearly so peculiar as that of St. Helena, as I am informed by Dr. Hooker, of Juan Fernandez. The peculiarity of the Galapageian Flora is best shown in certain families;—thus there are 21 species of Compositæ, of which 20 are peculiar to this archipelago; these belong to twelve genera, and of these genera no less than ten are confined to the archipelago! Dr. Hooker informs me that the Flora has an undoubted Western American character; nor can he detect in it any affinity with that of the Pacific. If, therefore, we except the eighteen marine, the one fresh-water, and one land-shell, which have apparently come here as colonists from the central islands of the Pacific, and likewise the one distinct Pacific species of the Galapageian group of finches, we see that this archipelago, though standing in the Pacific Ocean, is zoologically part of America.

If this character were owing merely to immigrants from America, there would be little remarkable in it; but we see that a vast majority of all the land animals, and that more than half of the flowering plants, are aboriginal productions. It was most striking to be surrounded by new birds, new reptiles, new shells, new insects, new plants, and yet by innumerable trifling details of structure, and even by the tones of voice and plumage of the birds, to have the temperate plains of Patagonia, of the hot dry deserts of Northern Chile, vividly brought before my eyes. Why, on these small points of land, which within a late geological period must have been covered by the ocean, which are formed of basaltic lava, and therefore differ in geological character from the American continent, and which are placed under a peculiar climate,—why were their aboriginal inhabitants, associated, I may add, in different proportions both in kind and number from those on the continent, and therefore acting on each other in a different manner—why were they created on American types of organization? It is probable that the islands of the Cape de Verd group resemble, in all their physical conditions, far more closely the Galapagos Islands than these latter physically resemble the coast of America; yet the aboriginal inhabitants of the two groups are totally unlike; those of the Cape de Verd Islands bearing the impress of Africa, as the inhabitants of the Galapagos Archipelago are stamped with that of America.

I have not as yet noticed by far the most remarkable feature in the natural history of this archipelago; it is, that the different islands to a considerable extent are inhabited by a different set of beings. My attention was first called to this fact by the Vice-Governor, Mr. Lawson, declaring that the tortoises differed from the different islands, and that he could with certainty tell from which island any one was brought. I did not for some time pay sufficient attention to this statement, and I had already partially mingled together the collections from two of the islands. I never dreamed that islands, about fifty or sixty miles apart, and most of them in sight of each other, formed of precisely the same rocks, placed under a quite similar climate, rising to a nearly equal height, would have been differently tenanted; but we shall soon see that this is the case. It is the fate of most voyagers, no sooner to discover what is most interesting in any locality, than they are hurried from it; but I ought, perhaps, to be thankful that I obtained sufficient materials to establish this most remarkable fact in the distribution of organic beings.

The inhabitants, as I have said, state that they can distinguish the tortoises from the different islands; and that they differ not only in size, but in other characters. Captain Porter has described those from Charles and from the nearest island to it, namely, Hood Island, as having their shells in front thick and turned up like a Spanish saddle, whilst the tortoises from James Island are rounder, blacker, and have a better taste when cooked. M. Bibron, moreover, informs me that he has seen what he considers two distinct species of tortoise from the Galapagos, but he does not know from which islands. The specimens that I brought from three islands were young ones; and probably owing to this cause, neither Mr. Gray nor myself could find in them any specific differences. I have remarked that the marine Amblyrhynchus was larger at Albemarle Island than elsewhere; and M. Bibron informs me that he has seen two distinct aquatic species of this genus; so that the different islands probably have their representative species or races of the Amblyrhynchus, as well as of the tortoise. My attention was first thoroughly aroused, by comparing together the numerous specimens, shot by myself and several other parties on board, of the mocking-thrushes, when, to my astonishment, I discovered that all those from Charles Island belonged to one species (Mimus trifasciatus); all from Albemarle Island to M. parvulus; and all from James and Chatham Islands (between which two other islands are situated, as connecting links) belonged to M. melanotis. These two latter species are closely allied, and would by some ornithologists be considered as only well-marked races or varieties; but the Mimus trifasciatus is very distinct. Unfortunately most of the specimens of the finch tribe were mingled together; but I have strong reasons to suspect that some of the species of the sub-group Geospiza are confined to separate islands. If the different islands have their representatives of Geospiza, it may help to explain the singularly large number of the species of this sub-group in this one small archipelago, and as a probable consequence of their numbers, the perfectly graduated series in the size of their beaks. Two species of the sub-group Cactornis, and two of Camarhynchus, were procured in the archipelago; and of the numerous specimens of these two sub-groups shot by four collectors at James Island, all were found to belong to one species of each; whereas the numerous specimens shot either on Chatham or Charles Island (for the two sets were mingled together) all belonged to the two other species: hence we may feel almost sure that these islands possess their representative species of these two sub-groups. In land-shells this law of distribution does not appear to hold good. In my very small collection of insects, Mr. Waterhouse remarks, that of those which were ticketed with their locality, not one was common to any two of the islands.

If we now turn to the Flora, we shall find the aboriginal plants of the different islands wonderfully different. I give all the following results on the high authority of my friend Dr. J. Hooker. I may premise that I indiscriminately collected everything in flower on the different islands, and fortunately kept my collections separate. Too much confidence, however, must not be placed in the proportional results, as the small collections brought home by some other naturalists, though in some respects confirming the results, plainly show that much remains to be done in the botany of this group: the Leguminosæ, moreover, have as yet been only approximately worked out: (see p173)

Hence we have the truly wonderful fact, that in James Island, of the thirty-eight Galapageian plants, or those found in no other part of the world, thirty are exclusively confined to this one island; and in Albemarle Island, of the twenty-six aboriginal Galapageian plants, twenty-two are confined to this one island, that is, only four are at present known to grow in the other islands of the archipelago; and so on, as shown in the

Name of Island	Total No. of Species	No. of Species found in other parts of the world	No. of Species confined to the Galapagos Archipelago	No. confined to the one Island	No. of Species confined to the Galapagos Archipelago, but found on more than the one Island
James Island	71	33	38	30	8
Albemarle Island	46	18	26	22	4
Chatham Island	32	16	16	12	4
Charles Island	68	39*	29	21	8

*(or 29, if the probably imported plants be subtracted)

above table, with plants from Chatham and Charles Islands. This fact will, perhaps, be rendered even more striking, by giving a few illustrations:—thus, Scalesia, a remarkable arborescent genus of the Compositæ, is confined to the archipelago: it has six species; one from Chatham, one from Albemarle, one from Charles Island, two from James Island, and the sixth from one of the three latter islands, but it is not known from which: not one of these six species grows on any two islands. Again, Euphorbia, a mundane or widely distributed genus, has here eight species, of which seven are confined to the archipelago, and not one found on any two islands: Acalypha and Borreria, both mundane genera, have respectively six and seven species, none of which have the same species on two islands, with the exception of one Borreria, which does occur on two islands. The species of the Compositæ are particularly local; and Dr. Hooker has furnished me with several other most striking illustrations of the difference of the species on the different islands. He remarks that this law of distribution holds good both with those genera confined to the archipelago, and those distributed in other quarters of the world: in like manner we have seen that the different islands have their proper species of the mundane genus of tortoise, and of the widely distributed American genus of the mocking-thrush, as well as of two of the Galapageian sub-groups of finches, and almost certainly of the Galapageian genus Amblyrhynchus.

The distribution of the tenants of this archipelago would not be nearly so wonderful, if, for instance, one island had a mocking-thrush, and a second island some other quite distinct genus; —if one island had its genus of lizard, and a second island another distinct genus, or none whatever;—or if the different islands were inhabited, not by representative species of the same genera of plants, but by totally different genera, as does to a certain extent hold good; for, to give one instance, a large berry-bearing tree at James Island has no representative species in Charles Island. But it is the circumstance, that several of the islands possess their own species of the tortoise, mocking-thrush, finches, and numerous plants, these species having the same general habits, occupying analogous situations, and obviously filling the same place in the natural economy of this archipelago, that strikes me with wonder. It may be suspected that some of these representative species, at least in the case of the tortoise and of some of the birds, may hereafter prove to be only well-marked races; but this would be of equally great interest to the philosophical naturalist. I have said that most of the islands are in sight of each other: I may specify that Charles Island is fifty miles from the nearest part of Chatham Island, and thirty-three miles from the nearest part of Albemarle Island. Chatham Island is sixty miles from the nearest part of James Island, but there are two intermediate islands between them which were not visited by me. James Island is only ten miles from the nearest part of Albemarle Island, but the two points where the collections were made are thirty-two miles apart. I must repeat, that neither the nature of the soil, nor height of the land, nor the climate, nor the general character of the associated beings, and therefore their action one on another, can differ much in the different islands. If there be any sensible difference in their climates, it must be between the windward group (namely Charles and Chatham Islands), and that to leeward; but there seems to be no corresponding difference in the productions of these two halves of the archipelago.

The only light which I can throw on this remarkable difference in the inhabitants of the different islands, is, that very strong currents of the sea running in a westerly and W.N.W. direction must separate, as far as transportal by the sea is concerned, the southern islands from the northern ones; and between these northern islands a strong N.W. current was observed, which must effectually separate James and Albemarle Islands. As the archipelago is free to a most remarkable degree from gales of wind, neither the birds, insects, nor lighter seeds, would be blown from island to island. And lastly, the profound depth of the ocean between the islands, and their apparently recent (in a geological sense) volcanic origin, render it highly unlikely that they were ever united; and this, probably, is a far more important consideration than any other, with respect to the geographical distribution of their inhabitants. Reviewing the facts here given, one is astonished at the amount of creative force, if such an expression may be used, displayed on these small, barren, and rocky islands; and still more so, at its diverse yet analogous action on points so near each other. I have said that the Galapagos Archipelago might be called a satellite attached to America, but it should rather be called a group of satellites, physically similar, organically distinct, yet intimately related to each other, and all related in a marked, though much lesser degree, to the great American continent.

I will conclude my description of the natural history of these islands, by giving an account of the extreme tameness of the birds.

This disposition is common to all the terrestrial species; namely, to the mocking-thrushes, the finches, wrens, tyrant-fly-catchers, the dove, and carrion-buzzard. All of them often approached sufficiently near to be killed with a switch, and sometimes, as I myself tried, with a cap or hat. A gun is here almost superfluous; for with the muzzle I pushed a hawk off the branch of a tree. One day, whilst lying down, a mocking-thrush lighted on the edge of a pitcher, made of the shell of a tortoise, which I held in my hand, and began very quietly to sip the water; it allowed me to lift it from the ground whilst seated on the vessel: I often tried, and very nearly succeeded, in catching these birds by their legs. Formerly the birds appear to have been even tamer than at present. Cowley (in the year 1684) says that the "Turtle-doves were so tame, that they would often

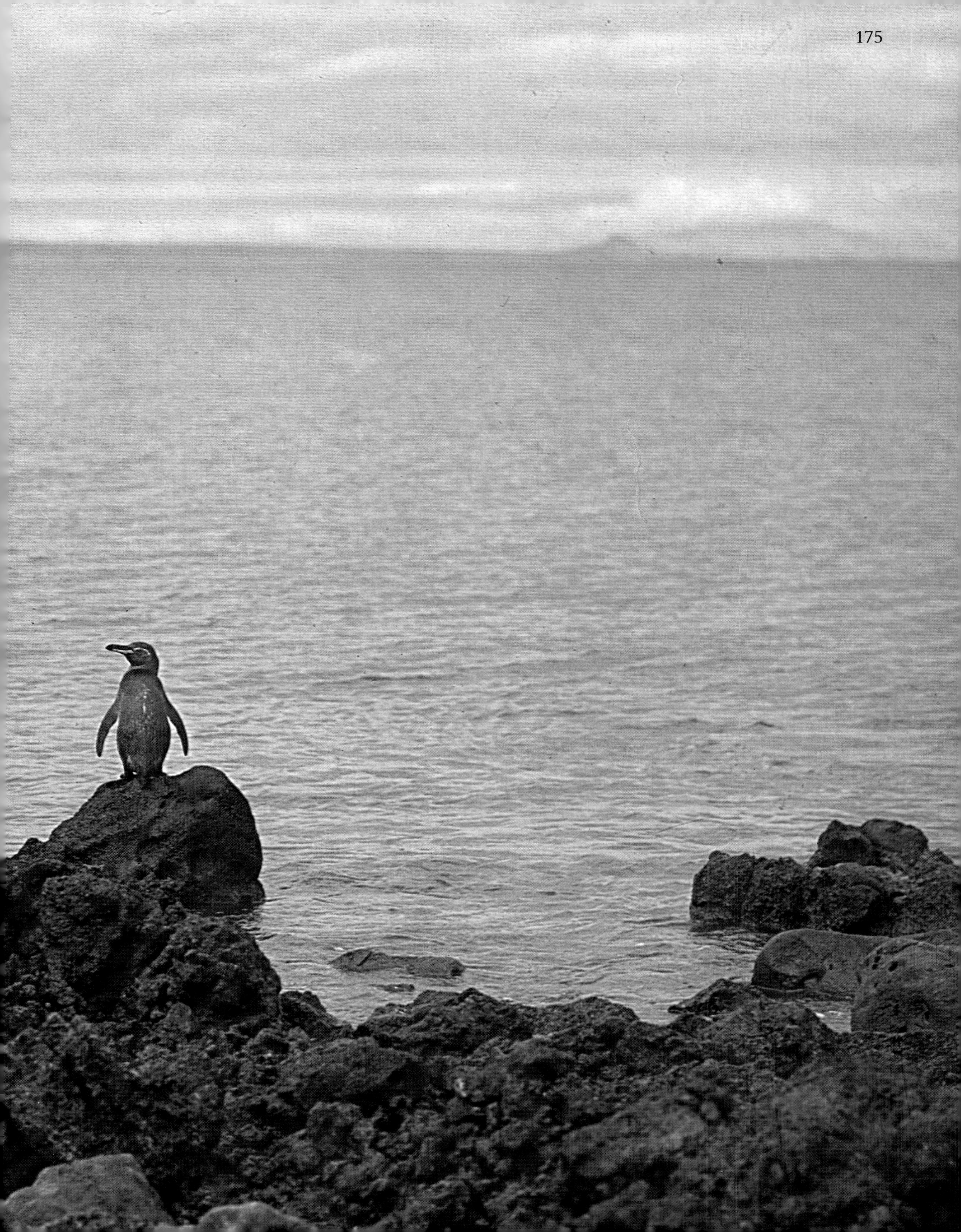

alight upon our hats and arms, so as that we could take them alive: they not fearing man, until such time as some of our company did fire at them, whereby they were rendered more shy." Dampier also, in the same year, says that a man in a morning's walk might kill six or seven dozen of these doves. At present, although certainly very tame, they do not alight on people's arms, nor do they suffer themselves to be killed in such large numbers. It is surprising that they have not become wilder; for these islands during the last hundred and fifty years have been frequently visited by bucaniers and whalers; and the sailors, wandering through the woods in search of tortoises, always take cruel delight in knocking down the little birds.

These birds, although now still more persecuted, do not readily become wild: in Charles Island, which had then been colonized about six years, I saw a boy sitting by a well with a switch in his hand, with which he killed the doves and finches as they came to drink. He had already procured a little heap of them for his dinner; and he said that he had constantly been in the habit of waiting by this well for the same purpose. It would appear that the birds of this archipelago, not having as yet learnt that man is a more dangerous animal than the tortoise or the Amblyrhynchus, disregard him, in the same manner as in England shy birds, such as magpies, disregard the cows and horses grazing in our fields.

The Falkland Islands offer a second instance of birds with a similar disposition. The extraordinary tameness of the little Opetiorhynchus has been remarked by Pernety, Lesson, and other voyagers. It is not, however, peculiar to that bird: the Polyborus, snipe, upland and lowland goose, thrush, bunting, and even some true hawks, are all more or less tame. As the birds are so tame there, where foxes, hawks, and owls occur, we may infer that the absence of all rapacious animals at the Galapagos, is not the cause of their tameness here. The upland geese at the Falklands show, by the precaution they take in building on the islets, that they are aware of their danger from the foxes; but they are not by this rendered wild towards man. This tameness of the birds, especially of the waterfowl, is strongly contrasted with the habits of the same species in Tierra del Fuego, where for ages past they have been persecuted by the wild inhabitants. In the Falklands, the sportsman may sometimes kill more of the upland geese in one day than he can carry home; whereas in Tierra del Fuego, it is nearly as difficult to kill one, as it is in England to shoot the common wild goose.

In the time of Pernety (1763), all the birds there appear to have been much tamer than at present; he states that the Opetiorhynchus would almost perch on his finger; and that with a wand he killed ten in half an hour. At that period the birds must have been about as tame, as they now are at the Galapagos. They appear to have learnt caution more slowly at these latter islands than at the Falklands, where they have had proportionate means of experience; for besides frequent visits from vessels, those islands have been at intervals colonized during the entire period. Even formerly, when all the birds were so tame, it was impossible by Pernety's account to kill the black-necked swan —a bird of passage, which probably brought with it the wisdom learnt in foreign countries.

I may add that, according to Du Bois, all the birds at Bourbon in 1571–72, with the exception of the flamingoes and geese, were so extremely tame, that they could be caught by the hand, or killed in any number with a stick. Again, at Tristan d'Acunha in the Atlantic, Carmichael states that the only two land-birds, a thrush and a bunting, were "so tame as to suffer themselves to be caught with a hand-net." From these several facts we may, I think, conclude, first, that the wilderness of birds with regard to man, is a particular instinct directed against *him*, and not dependent on any general degree of caution arising from other sources of danger; secondly, that it is not acquired by individual birds in a short time, even when much persecuted; but that in the course of successive generations it becomes hereditary. With domesticated animals we are accustomed to see new mental habits or instincts acquired and rendered hereditary; but with animals in a state of nature, it must always be most difficult to discover instances of acquired hereditary knowledge. In regard to the wildness of birds towards man, there is no way of accounting for it, except as an inherited habit: comparatively few young birds, in any one year, have been injured by man in England, yet almost all, even nestlings, are afraid of him; many individuals, on the other hand, both at the Galapagos and at the Falklands, have been pursued and injured by man, but yet have not learned a salutary dread of him. We may infer from these facts, what havoc the introduction of any new beast of prey must cause in a country, before the instincts of the indigenous inhabitants have become adapted to the stranger's craft or power.

The Galapagos Archipelago

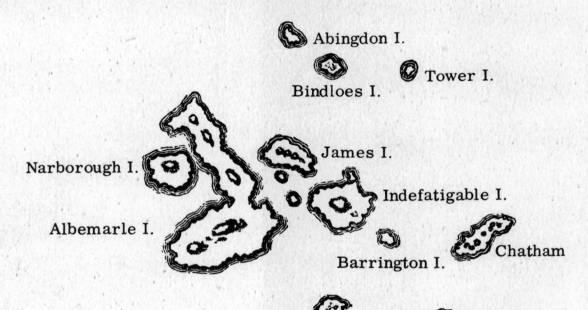

Culpepper I.

Wenman I.

60 Miles

Abingdon I.

Bindloes I.

Tower I.

Narborough I.

James I.

Indefatigable I.

Albemarle I.

Barrington I.

Chatham

Charles I.

Hood's I